AMERICAN VULGAR

ROBERT GRUDIN

AMERICAN VULGAR

The Politics of Manipulation versus the Culture of Awareness

SHOEMAKER HOARD

Excerpt from Mary Gordon's "How Ireland Hid Its Dirt Laundry" copyright © 2003 by The New York Times Co.; excerpt from Erica Goode's "The Gorge Yourself Environment" copyright © 2003 by The New York Times Co.; excerpt from Warren St. John's "On the Final Journey, One Size Doesn't Fit All" copyright © 2003 by The New York Times Co.; excerpt from Kate Zernike's "Fight Against Fat Shifts to the Workplace" copyright © 2003 by The New York Times Co.; excerpt from Frank Rich's "The Wiretappers that Couldn't Shoot Straight" copyright © 2006 by The New York Times Co. All reprinted with permission. Every effort has been made to secure permissions. We regret any inadvertent omission.

Library of Congress Cataloging-in-Publication Data
Grudin, Robert.
American vulgar : the politics of manipulation versus the culture of awareness / Robert Grudin.
p. cm.
Includes bibliographical references.
ISBN-13: 978-1-59376-102-8
ISBN-10: 1-59376-102-3
1. Vulgarity-Social aspects-United States. 2. Mass media-Social aspects-United States. 3. Popular culture-United States. 4. Political culture-United States. 5. Ignorance (Theory of knowledge)-Social aspects. 6. Consciousness-Social aspects. 7. Awareness-Social aspects. 8. Social psychology-United States. I. Title.
HN59.2.G78 2006
306.0973-dc22   2006008709

Book design by David Bullen Design
Printed in the United States of America

Shoemaker & Hoard
An Imprint of Avalon Publishing Group, Inc.

1400 65th Street, Suite 250
Emeryville, CA 94608
Distributed by Publishers Group West

10 9 8 7 6 5 4 3 2 1

To Michaela Paasche Grudin

CONTENTS

A WAR AND A KILLING

From mid-March to mid-April 2003, the American viewing public doubled in size as television cameras brought a live war into their living rooms. Attention flagged only slightly as Baghdad fell and the Coalition turned its attention to less important cities in the North, but when these too surrendered, it was clear to media executives that their newfound market share might be subject to serious erosion. Accordingly, decisions were made in high places, correspondents hopped on planes, and all of a sudden, completely new images danced on the daytime screen. These images were no longer of a war that killed thousands and changed international history. They were now of a woman named Laci Peterson, once young and pretty, whose headless body had been found in San Francisco Bay.

The switch from honorable reportage to yellow journalism was dumbfounding. Journalists missed no opportunity to pander to the baser instincts of their constituency: to the voyeurism that had been so gainfully exploited in the Simpson murder case, to the ghoulishness that makes millions of dollars for horror movies, to the zest for violence that draws large audiences to televised contact sports and crime dramas. Though it was never shown graphically, Ms. Peterson's headless corpse became a national product, boosting ratings and selling ads. The TV channels made money. But they vulgarized their viewers in the process.

A far deeper national embarrassment is now apparent. As I write in 2006, the Iraqi war itself, billed as a defense of liberty in the face of mounting terrorism, has emerged as an arbitrary initiative, based on specious allegations and advanced with inadequate intelligence. In late 2005, as American opposition to the war broke the surface on several fronts, George W. Bush and his aides compounded their lies by falsely asserting that, before the war, they had given Congress all the intelligence that they had received from their own classified sources. If distracting the public with murder and corpses amounts to vulgarization, what can we say about an administration that goes to war blindfolded and thrives on the public's ignorance of its motives?

What follows is a meditation on American vulgarity: its components, its causes, and its possible cures. I realize that Americans tend to be uneasy with the V-word, usually linking it to the snotty tastes of some ancien régime. My response to this is that only the word *vulgarity* can describe the particular combination of gullibility, ignorance, and self-indulgence that characterizes the American marketplace, and only the word *vulgarizing* can describe the various hucksters who manipulate public choice. I also believe that the real opposite of vulgarity is not some highbrow notion of sophistication (a word already vulgarized by marketers), but rather consciousness, pure and simple. Consciousness, the ability to be alert to important things and literate in them, is a kind of mental oxygen: an element without which people lose track of their own lives, and societies cannot renew themselves. Consciousness, to be sure, has its liabilities. When we focus only on the vulgarity of others, and without self-scrutiny, our consciousness can be as dangerous as ignorance. Figures as well known as Virginia Woolf, H. G. Wells, and D. H. Lawrence have erred in this direction (see Chapter 9). But consciousness is well worth the risk, especially in times like these, when essential liberties—including even our access to information—are threatened by corporate greed and political interest. And, as we will see from the experience of civil rights activist Frederick Douglass, the first subject of our consciousness should be the extent to which our own lives are being degraded.

As this book has its goats, it also has its heroes: individuals who attempt to restore rationality to practices that have been corrupted. You will not be surprised to see environmentalists and journalists among them; less likely champions, however, include a Berkeley businesswoman, a German lit professor, a D.C. lawyer, and an analyst at the World Bank. Few if any of these are counterculture figures, and indeed a number of them endorse economic and cultural reform because it makes good business sense. I hope that they will serve as examples suggesting that vulgarity and the greed that feeds it are not irreversible conditions, and that the same liberty that allows for vulgarity holds the hope of renewed awareness.

This book is divided into two sections. Because vulgarity is a relatively unfamiliar lens through which to view American culture, Part 1 will address in detail the many ways in which marketers, media, and politicians are profiting from the debasement of American sensibilities. Part 2 will examine consciousness in similar detail, focusing on the history of consciousness in Western culture and the sources of consciousness in education, literature, and the give-and-take of real-world experience. In other words, Part 1 will show off American Vulgar in all its gaudy splendor, and Part 2 will give American Vulgar a run for its money.

As you will note almost from the outset, this book is not a typical work of research. In an effort to get as close as possible to the pulse of American culture in real time, I have consulted not only printed books but newspapers, television, the radio, the Internet, and e-mail. This sort of research had the upside of keeping me more up-to-date—sometimes by years—than I would have been in a print culture. But the downside is that many of my sources are at best fragile and impermanent. In order to compensate as much as possible for this disadvantage, I have quoted at length from some Web pages in my notes.

Part One

———

VULGARITY AND AMERICAN CULTURE

———

CHAPTER ONE

THE DOMAINS
OF VULGARITY

In general people will talk and write about everything in the world except the most important things, and they will skip the most important things because they are quite unaware of them, and this unawareness is precisely what makes these things the most important. In old-fashioned aristocracies like Europe of the eighteenth century, the most important things included the unconscionable arrogance shown by the ruling class towards the people beneath them. The gradually dawning recognition of this injustice led to the fall of empire. In modern democracy and particularly in America, the most important things include the vulgarization of the populace, fostered by the mass market, politicians, churches, the media, and even the educational system. If the "specter brooding over Europe" in 1848 was oppression, it is now vulgarity, in a thousand intrusive forms, that broods over and threatens the Land of the Free.

What is vulgarity? Synonyms like *grossness* or *baseness* only beg the question: what makes an action vulgar, gross, or base? My working definition is as follows: An action is vulgar when it is at once ignorant, harmful, and popular.[1] And vulgarization is any process in which public awareness is stifled in the interests of state power or private profit.

I must add that the ignorance involved in vulgarity is compound. To act vulgarly we must be ignorant not only of other people but of ourselves, not only of the nature of our action but of its ramifications in the world at large. To act vulgarly we must, with the aid of willing marketers, politicians, and priests, indulge our own ignorance in large, mutually supportive groups. Vulgarity reaches full bloom when it becomes established practice and takes on the look of law. It then becomes something worse than ignorance: a kind of communal depression.

By vulgarity, moreover, I mean not only specific offenses to taste like gambling casinos, fast food, TV evangelism, and professional wrestling. I mean also the comprehensive cultural laxity that spawns such monstrosities, making them not only routine but overpowering, and simultaneously blinding us to their dangers. This laxity is fed by a corporate system that has abandoned long-term development in favor of quarterly profits, by media whose moral standards are based on viewer share, and by a system of higher education that has sold out its image of the humanities and critical thinking as the main bases for consciousness and values. America is being vulgarized from the top down.

As an instance of profit-driven vulgarization, consider the cigarette smoker in the 1970s. Smoking was allowed in restaurants, on airliners, in stores and offices, virtually everywhere. It was no surprise to see somebody lighting up during the course of a meal. It was common to see groups of three or four people lighting up at once as though performing a ritual. Smokers in those innocent days had no solid knowledge that their smoking led to lung cancer, caused heart or respiratory disease, had dangerous secondary health effects on others, or produced clinical addiction. Neither had doctors, legislators, or journalists. The only people gaining solid knowledge were scientists funded by groups like the American Cancer Society and the tobacco companies themselves, whose researchers, behind closed doors, were determining beyond doubt that cigarettes were slow poison. And the tobacco companies were not telling anybody a thing about this. In order to keep making money, they not only had to keep killing their customers, but had to vulgarize them in the process.

Also consider, as a non-American but highly edifying example, the locus classicus of the establishment-driven debasement of culture: the Third Reich. Adolf Hitler consistently appealed to his people's basest instincts: fear, anger, and the desire for control. At the same time that he was diverting mass frustration into hatred towards Jews, gypsies, and foreigners, he was glamorizing his war machine until it symbolically radiated an aura of transcendent power. These acts, plus his flooding all of Germany's information channels with atrocious lies, contributed to the most effective vulgarization of a citizenry in modern times. Hannah Arendt missed the mark when she called Nazi evil "banal." *Banal* is a philosopher's word, devoid of real-world meaning. *Banal* does not get into the disgust of evil, the body odor of evil, the rich stink of it. More accurately put, Hitler and the Nazis were monstrously vulgar.[2]

Why should I claim that vulgarization particularly threatens Americans? In the first place, because it almost always *has*. American lack of savoir faire and self-knowledge has been a European refrain since the eighteenth century. In 2003 Simon Schama collected a bouquet of anti-American diatribes and published them, presumably as a corrective to the outbursts of patriotic slogans that followed 9/11. The themes of self-importance and provincialism recur in most of Schama's collection. Thus, British visitor Frances Trollope describes this American self-conceit:

> If the citizens of the United States were indeed the devoted patriots they call themselves, they would surely not thus encrust themselves in the hard, dry, stubborn persuasion, that they are the first and best of the human race, that nothing is to be learnt, but what they are able to teach, and that nothing is worth having, which they do not possess.

America's lack of self-awareness was seen to result in alarming self-contradictions. Schama quotes the English radical Thomas Day, who wrote in 1776:

> If there be an object truly ridiculous in nature, it is an American patriot, signing resolutions of independency [sic] with the one hand, and with the other brandishing a whip over his affrighted slaves.

Schama adds his own critique of American self-righteousness:

> Just as obnoxious as the fraud of liberty was the fraud of Christian piety, a finger-jabbing rectitude incapable of asserting a policy without invoking the Deity as a co-sponsor. This hallelujah Republic was a bedlam of hymns and hosannas, but the only true church was the church of the Dollar Almighty. And how could the cult of individualism be taken seriously when it had produced a society that set such great store by conformity?[3]

Certainly, Schama's broadside is heavy-handed. America makes up, in abundant human capital, for what it may lack in polish. And certainly, over the last 140 years, Europeans have brutalized and debased each other dozens of times, while there has not been a tyranny or a war in North America. But the European critique of America is nothing if not consistent. When we are criticized by Europeans, it is usually for vulgarity.

What are the roots of this vulgarity? The only European culture that is often derided as vulgar is that of Germany. America and Germany have much in common. Both infrastructures are concentrated on technology, production, mercantilism, and finance. Both have become hothouses for materialism and its vulgarizing effects. And both are predominantly Protestant countries, graced with the moral earnestness (often bordering on myopic self-righteousness) of the Protestant tradition. The only major difference is America's lifelong and unswerving dedication to liberty, which has not only thrust the United States to the apex of world power but also opened wide our gates to a bedlam of mass-market vulgarities. As Americans are free to elect their governments and express their views, so too are they free to indulge their own ignorance and enrich the clowns, quacks, and hucksters who help them do so.

To appreciate the variety, scope, and robustness of American vulgarity, let us briefly visit nine of its most visible domains: violence, idolatry, anger and hatred, superstition, addiction, machismo, voyeurism, the cult of money, and ignorance.

Violence. Americans have long followed, and lavishly funded, violent sports like American football, hockey, boxing, and wrestling. Automobile racing, with its deafening noise and potential for major mayhem, is one of the nation's greatest sources of television revenue. European visitors, who are more used to soccer and tennis, are routinely shocked by all this roughness, as Schama reports:

> Likewise, the appeal of American football—the Harvard-Yale game became almost as much a fixture of foreign itineraries as the stockyards—was explicable only as quasi-Spartan military training. What really startled Europeans was the blood-lust the sport seemed to provoke in spectators. At one Harvard-Yale game, Huret listened in appalled fascination as a nineteen-year-old yelled "Kill him!" and "Break his neck!" from the bleachers.

America's penchant for heavy hits is also indulged in Hollywood movies and television series about police officers, private eyes, and emergency rooms.

To see exactly how gross things can get, you might have tuned in to Fox's 2002 sports phenomenon, *Celebrity Boxing*. These matches feature well-known people who are silly or desperate enough to put on gloves and batter away at each other on cable TV. James Poniewozik of *Time* thus describes one of Fox's major matchups, a bout between ice skater Tonya Harding and Clinton accuser Paula Jones:

> Harding was the heavy favorite, and the crowd went wild the few times Jones landed a punch. But by the second round, the woman who nearly brought down a president was running away from Harding, seemingly in tears. To her credit, she made it to round three, when she miserably asked for the fight to be stopped—while Harding came up and popped her anyway, in the back of the head. The crowd booed, but Tonya's probably immune to that by now, and she accepted her win with what was probably the closest to graciousness she's ever come: "I knocked her down a few times," she said. "That's all that matters."[4]

As coarse as participation in *Celebrity Boxing* may be, it pales by comparison with the coarseness of its audience, who presumably turn it on, not to enjoy athletic excellence, but to see people, and especially female people, visit violence upon each other. To think about this sort of viewing public, and the greedy producers who pander to it, is to grow slightly wistful about the more constrained pursuits of nations overseas.

Idolatry. A regular feature of medieval legend is the so-called familiar demon, a fiend who, in human or animal form, attaches himself to an evildoer, haunting his or her every step. Such demons drum up business for the Devil, frequently encouraging human beings to cultivate the vices that will lead them to perdition. Paradoxically and disturbingly, these demons represent both crime and punishment. Every aspect of American vulgarity is haunted by just such a demon. But the evil spirits are not called demons by name. They are called marketers.

Take, for example, idolatry. The worship of images and personages goes back to the dawn of history and is a firmly established form of vulgarity. Americans, who are traditionally supposed to be immune to idolatry ("Live free or die," "Don't tread on me") are in fact its most enthusiastic practitioners, and they are catered to by media who earn solid profits from their customers' foolishness. Some forms of idolatry, as in "the King" and "Blue Eyes," are blatant and easily caricatured. Others, like the sale and use of religious symbols, carry the stamp of propriety. Still others masquerade as sophistication.

Sophisticate idolatry? Stranger things have happened. Look at the *New York Times* Best Seller List (it doesn't matter much which one). Among the formula novels, diet books, and bourgeois travel memoirs, you will find a steady stream of celebrity biographies that purport to give intimate access into the lives of public idols. The fate of one such book, Richard Blow's 2002 biography of his former *George* Magazine colleague, John F. Kennedy, Jr., can tell us something about idolatry and its market. First, big publishing turned down an earlier proposal for a Kennedy biography on the grounds that it was indecorously premature (a sign that U.S. book publishers like their vulgarity served cold). Second, when the Blow biography finally appeared, other Kennedy associates alleged that it had been produced under morally compromised conditions:

> The organizers said that they wanted to register a protest of what they called Mr. Blow's exploitation of Mr. Kennedy's death for personal gain. Mr. Blow, they said, had initially barred anyone on the magazine's staff from talking about Mr. Kennedy to the news media, but then reversed himself to sell the rights to his own book on him.[5]

Does this mean that said associates had not been interested in personal gain themselves? All this sounds less like respectable publishing than like thieves squabbling over loot. But living with an idol inevitably imposes guilty temptations, and this is true partly because the idol is not a normal human being but rather a media-manipulated icon.

Anger and Hatred. Anger and hatred are associated with vulgarity because they are robotic emotions, immune to consideration or dialogue, and because they are neighbors to violence. People with communicative skills can sort things out without hard feelings or violent confrontations; good communicators can practice leadership skills to achieve their goals. Vulgarians, on the other hand, can only fume and shout. Their threatening behavior suggests hidden feelings of impotence and frustration.

But tyrants and marketers can turn anger into a cash crop. Hitler could not have come to power had he not transformed public frustration into anger against Jews and foreign powers. For years, he was able to funnel his own ill temper, which was pathological, into fiery, statist rhetoric. Anger merchants in the United States, including Senator Joseph McCarthy and the Republicans who tried to impeach President Bill Clinton, have not produced as many fireworks. America, even America at its worst, is too happy a nation to buckle into a fit of rage.

Troubling, nonetheless, is the effort to market anger as a product in public dialogue and news. Here is Michael Savage of MSNBC excoriating a viewer who dared to criticize him: "Moron! Moron! Moron! . . . Gargle with Rogaine! Grow a beard on your tongue!"[6] Talk show hosts like Jerry Springer have regularly imported anger into the radio and television marketplace. The conservative news channel, Fox, mounted a campaign to stir up anger against citizens who were critical of the war in Iraq. This use of anger is destructive for a number of reasons. It blurs issues. It polarizes. It delays resolution, freezing progress. Most seriously, however, it is a baldly cynical appeal to the worst of human failings. The mass-marketing of anger, especially with regard to complex political issues, is a dangerous debasement of public sensibilities.

Superstition. American superstition is a huge financial garden tended by national tabloids full of UFOs, ghost stories, and stone circles. The U.S. circulation of the *National Inquirer* is 6 million, making the tabloid's popularity greater than that of *Time* Magazine (4.2 million), figures suggesting that a substantial block of the American reading public prefers to be systematically misinformed. But far more epidemic and menacing is the role of superstition in organized religion. Religion degenerates into superstition when names like Jesus and Allah are hawked as heal-alls whose absolute power absolves the worshiper of onerous duties like education and personal responsibility. Religion degenerates into superstition when priests capitalize, in power and money, on the unquestioning faith of their parishioners. Religion degenerates into superstition when faith is turned into fuel for war and outrage.

The terrorist attacks by Islamic militants, now current, are evidence of the alarming potential of superstition. The suicide bombers have been taught, and believe it as gospel, that on death they will go straight into paradise and obtain, in abundance and perpetuity, the sexual favors of gorgeous maidens.[7] This sort of education has got to be reviewed if there is to be any stability in the Middle East. But we should also review any sect, Eastern or Western, that limits its adherents' intellectual growth, or any leader who, like President George W. Bush, exploits religious faith for political gain. And we must be particularly vigilant against right-wing efforts to turn America, a nation founded on the rule of reason, into a religious oligarchy.

By the way, campaigning against idolatry and superstition in your own sect need not turn you into the neighborhood atheist. Earlier critics of these vulgarities included Jeremiah, Jesus, and Francis of Assisi.

Addictions. Vulgarity does not discriminate in terms of race or sex or class. Like the sun, vulgarity shines on rich and poor alike. It inheres in any individual who defaults to the easiest course, who addresses all issues in the short term, who resorts to the preconceived solutions of a prevailing idiom. If Donald Carnegie Vanderbilt Rockefeller III leaves his Veuve Cliquot bottles littering the beach, he is indulging in vulgarity. If presidential candidates run under the nicknames Jimmy, Bill, and Al, they are marketing vulgarity. When the president of the United States pronounces *nuclear* "nucular," he is chewing on vulgarity. But vulgar habits, and their attendant marketers, tend to cluster around social strata that are poorly informed, and hence vulgarity often takes on the trappings of class.

This is particularly true of vulgarities related to addiction. Check out your nearest casino, and you are likely to find three of the cardinal vulgarities—smoking, drinking, and gambling—indulged in by a consumer population that knows and cares for little else. Move on to Vegas, and you will find these habits tended to by an organized-crime establishment that also traffics in heroine and cocaine. All the above are multibillion-dollar enterprises, focusing on working-class America, and together (with their victims' enthusiastic support), they prevent millions of Americans from achieving self-reliance or a better life.

An even more dangerous vulgarity—more dangerous because it presently affects three in five Americans—is overeating. Here as elsewhere, unhealthy and degenerative habits are fostered and maintained by a huge market. The food industry uses chemical strategies to make Americans eat more and more. A restaurant chef will tell you that almost any cooked dish, from fish stew to steak to veggies, can be improved in its flavor by a dollop of butter or cream. Such an addition is not healthy, of course, and it really isn't very good cooking, but it's a simple way to make things taste good.

But things are not quite as simple as that. Butter, cream, and other fatty foods do more than just taste good. Fat molecules latch on to receptor sites in our nerve cells, producing mild euphoria and a sense of calm. When fat is combined with sugar, as in ice cream, we get a double whammy, because sugar, a chemical cousin of alcohol, carries its own neurological punch. The psychological effects of fats and sugars are little different from the effects of alcohol, nicotine, or drugs. The use of fats and sugars can thus be part of a habit-forming commercial enticement.[8]

A conspiracy of chefs? Little chance of that. But project this analysis into the fast-food marketplace, and you will find the smoking gun. Fast-food marketers like McDonald's and the Colonel know exactly what they are doing when they pump fats and sugars down the communal gullet. They know that fats and sugars are habit-forming chemicals. Both fat and sugar are well-documented mood-enhancers:

> A low-fat diet may make you grumpy. British researchers assessed the moods of 20 people, ages 20–37, before and after eating either a daily total of 41 percent or 25 percent of calories from fat. After a month, the lower-fat eaters were rated as more hostile and depressed. Those on the higher-fat diet exhibited better moods and less tension and anxiety. One explanation: Fat stimulates hormones that influence activity of the brain chemical serotonin, important in governing mood. Low serotonin is linked with increased aggression and depression.[9]

But fast-food producers also know that fats and sugars, taken in quantity, are unhealthy.[10] These businesses know that their establishments are profiting from the addictive habits, health problems, and, in many cases, premature deaths of their customers. They know, finally, that their victims will be primarily blue-collar workers, who lack the money for expensive meals and the inclination to eat healthily. To keep this audience captive, marketers will routinely lie, claiming that their sugary products are low-fat or fat-free but knowing all the while that the body converts sugar to fat.[11]

Machismo. "A new pickup truck the size of a Boeing 747 cruises through a rural landscape, dwarfing everything else in sight. Its image breathes power and domination. Yes, there is big work at hand, but Monster Pickup will get the job done." In 2003, this TV commercial was beamed to households all over America by one of the Big Three automakers. The body language was clear enough. First, it was a warning shot against the Japanese competition, who were, at that time, mainly producing compact pickups. Second, it was an appeal to that element of American male psychology that craves control.

Be it expressed in beer ads, Harleys, martial arts, football, weaponry, or a variety of other guises, American Macho is a tried-and-true perversion catered to by major markets. Like food addiction, it is primarily a blue-collar or no-collar phenomenon, functioning perhaps as a psychological compensation for the sense of disempowerment that prevails in these classes. But like other forms of compensation, it does nothing to resolve the root issue or heal the frustration. Instead, the macho business makes things worse by draining the few household dollars that might have been invested in a better life.

But this, of course, is macho at its best. At its worst, it is criminal and perverted, fueling impulses too ugly to describe. The compulsion to control has long been documented as a principle of criminal psychology. The urge arises as an unhealthy substitute for aspiration: the normal desire to empower oneself in socially valuable ways. Individuals afflicted with the urge to control cannot relate to other people on equal terms; they must dominate or feel dominated. The act of controlling another person, as in rape or other violence, becomes a short-term gratification, generally leading to another cycle of frustration and violence.

Voyeurism. Like licensed Peeping Toms, Americans find nothing so edifying as live footage of the intimate secrets of strangers. The grosser, the better. At the outset, I referred to the U.S. media's indomitably vulgar treatment of the Laci Peterson murder case. This treatment had all the earmarks of a classic engorgement of voyeurism: contempt for the delicacy of family feelings, contempt for legal protocol, indulgence in sexual prurience, sadomasochism, human butchery, human decomposition. And the media displayed all the fake emotions by which voyeurism is conveyed as something genteel: shock, grief, pity, and passion for justice. The fate of Ms. Peterson, they would have it, was a terrible thing—so terrible that they chewed on it and lived off it for two years, so terrible that advertisers bled money for viewer share.

In what ways does the voyeurism market affect society? Spectacular coverage of violent crime has never been proven beneficial for younger viewers, and I doubt that any adult seriously believes that it is. When the media fixate on lurid topics like the Peterson case, important issues like terrorism, Palestinian statehood, globalization, and the environment get short shrift, while positive and educational news is all but ignored. Most egregiously, the viewing public is dragged down to its basest impulses, its psychological dirty underwear, where its nose is vigorously rubbed. These are the joys of vulgarity, and we are its beneficiaries.

The Cult of Money. American vulgarity is a mass-market phenomenon, which means that on the supply side, American vulgarity is about huge sums of money. Money is the sunlight that shines on the garden of vulgarity and the water that feeds its thirsty roots. Money is what makes tobacco and food companies poison their customers and what makes gaming houses and talk show hosts degrade their patrons. Two corollaries follow from this premise. First, providers who deemphasize money can rise above vulgarity. Second, money-based products and services, no matter how elegantly presented, will convey vulgarity from provider to client.

The first corollary can be illustrated by the experience of teachers in our public schools. Teachers are professionals in every sense of the word, except salary. The money line that produces their modest income does not come directly from their students, or even their students' families. Teachers have nothing to sell their students; on the contrary, teachers challenge their students to learn new things. Most importantly, the major rewards of teaching are not financial. Good teaching rises above vulgarity and, as it increases awareness, fights vulgarity in the bargain. The same may be said about any people who value professional excellence or service to society more than profit. They have engaged life. They have achieved what money cannot buy.

The second corollary is a moral dynamic that operates on every economic level. To say that the quest for money corrupts is only half of it, for questers after money cannot achieve their goal unless they also vulgarize their customers.

Take the following *New Yorker* ad from Phoenix Wealth Management. Three sassily dressed young people, two female, one male, all looking scandalously smug, lounge in an upscale wood-and-leather study that resembles a shop window. The laconic message in the upper left reads

Devoted children (Share of estate: 33%)

and in the upper right

Delighted alma mater (Share of estate: 67%)

with kind words about philanthropy and contact information below. We ask ourselves, how large does an estate have to be to make 11 percent a suitable bequest to a child brought up in the high style? $30 million total? Probably at minimum. This rough figure gives us the ad's target audience: no piddling million-plus midgets for us; we need solid, eight-figure trenchermen, or at least eight-figure wanna-bes. The ad's subtext is an unabashed paean to complacency and gross wealth. It's very nice to have an oak-and-leather study. It's very nice to have spoiled, bored kids who mainly "hang out" and dress like models. It's very nice to know that you will be wined and dined by a college president and that, maybe maybe, when the great Lender in the sky calls in your account, you will have the next best thing to sainthood, a hall on campus named after you. Best of all, it's supernice to be *stinking rich*, so rich that you can pay us a small fortune per year just for managing your loot.

The *New Yorker* itself, in fact, is something like Dr. Jekyll and Mr. Hyde. Its texts are highly presentable by journalistic standards. Its nonfiction articles treat their topics in depth and usually from independent perspectives. It is a strong source of information and a refreshing well of consciousness. But its major ads often sing another song. They sing not only to major-league money, but to people who want to imitate it or show it off. As in a $100 Rabbit corkscrew. A $195 Peretti shaving brush. A $325 razor. A "notebook" computer that resembles a real notebook in every respect except that it is heavier and costs a thousand times as much. A Cartier diamond goody so expensive that its price is decorously withheld. In a full-pager, auto-racing names Roger Penske and Sir Jackie Stewart face each other uncandidly in front of what looks like a pasted-in racetrack background. The idea is that the two men's "perpetual passion for racing" somehow rhymes with Rolex, two of whose eighteen-karat gold Cosmographs are pictured below. The ad does not specify a price (if you need to know, why bother?), but on the Internet, these watches are trading for $15,000—*used,* that is, and without warranty. The targeted customer: a baby boomer old enough to have been a Stewart fan, low-browed enough to admire auto racing, rich enough to shove thirty big ones across the counter, and, of course, vulgar enough to show off a gold Rolex. How many of those customers really exist? Quite a few, apparently. After all, this is the U.S. of A.[12]

Because these ads, for all their appeal to taste and class, virtually reek of dross, let's call them Elegant Vulgar. They are the way in which the mass market infiltrates Park Avenue and asserts itself at the apex of class. They are the raw hunger beneath the glitter, the raging angst beneath apparent calm. Their presence makes the *New Yorker* something like a philanthropist who finances her generous giving with night duty as a courtesan, or a stately white ocean liner powered by a grimy, slave-manned engine room. The ads' insistent presence in our benchmark publication is a timely reminder. You can run from American Vulgar, but you cannot hide.

Ignorance. Other aspects of vulgarity will be addressed in future chapters. Here let us turn to the granddaddy of all vulgarisms, ignorance. What sorts of ignorance? Ignorance of our freedom and our responsibility. Ignorance of the interests and perspectives of our fellow human beings. Ignorance of our environment. Ignorance of the enormous power of time and habit to liberate or enslave us. Ignorance of our own ignorance. Reasonable people recognize their own ignorance and use it as a goad to learning. Vulgarians retire into their burrows of ignorance and congratulate themselves on their wisdom.

Book publishing would seem to be the last refuge of real consciousness, but even here, there are signs of erosion. Remembering how the untimely death of John F. Kennedy, Jr., aroused a feeding frenzy of publishing vulgarity, let us look now at how a writer of fiction can mislead and debase millions of readers with the full approval of the cultural community.

From the spring of 2003 until the winter of 2004, Dan Brown's novel *The Da Vinci Code* stood at the top of national best-seller lists (by mid-2005, it had sold 10 million copies in hardcover). The novel derived its popularity not only from its fast-paced twists and turns but from its inside information about Vatican politics. Brown also makes notable use of Renaissance history, referring repeatedly to an alleged secret intellectual society called the Priory of Sion. The publishers claim that this research is accurate, and Brown repeated this claim on National Public Radio's *Weekend Edition—Saturday* on April 26, 2003. But the references to the Priory of Sion as a historical institution are bogus. The concept of a secret society named Sion was actually dreamed up in the early twentieth century by French ultra-rightists as a way of defaming Jews and Freemasons. The French group falsely averred that the Jews and Freemasons were involved in an international conspiracy. This slanderous hoax, published as *The Protocols of Zion*, was immensely successful—so much so that it was still being used in e-mail propaganda against Israel in recent years. In 1982, the French book became the basis for another specious best-seller, *Holy Blood, Holy Grail,* by Michael Baigent, Richard Leigh, and Henry Lincoln, a work of fictive revisionism that purported to show that Jesus Christ had sex with Mary Magdalen and sired the Merovingian kings. *Holy Blood, Holy Grail,* hoax and all, was apparently Dan Brown's historical source for *The Da Vinci Code.* Amazingly, neither he, his agent, his editor, nor Linda Wertheimer, who conducted the National Public Radio (NPR) interview, were aware of the abundant material incriminating *The Protocols of Zion* and the authors of *Holy Blood, Holy Grail.*[13]

Why is the Sion hoax so important? First, because it has done harm. Brown's "research," so unprofessionally executed, is being marketed as canon law and is unintentionally breathing new life into one of the most vicious and harmful slanders ever concocted. Second, the hoax is important because the cavalier attitude towards history that typifies this publishing venture is part of an epidemic relaxation of standards that today extends through publishing into the academy and discourse at large. Elsewhere, I have discussed an outright misstatement of history emanating from a highly visible academic authority, rubber-stamped by publishers, and pumped into the Western intellectual bloodstream.[14] Steven Spielberg's film *Munich* is an example of historical details being fictionalized and then touted as serious statements about history. And while the Internet was buzzing about this film's pros and cons, the same medium was also crackling about the suspect historicity of James

Frey's best-selling memoir, *A Million Little Pieces.* Given such questionable practices, it is perhaps no coincidence that since 2001, three well-known historians, all Americans, have been censured for falsehood or plagiarism.[15]

The 2006 trophy for the relentless pursuit of ignorance, however, belongs to the champions of so-called intelligent design (a variant of creationism). This transparent effort to bypass the U.S. Constitution and Christianize America's public schools was exposed in a December 2005 ruling made by Judge John Jones and summarized by *New York Times* reporter Laurie Goodstein:

> [Jones] concluded that intelligent design was not science, and that in order to claim that it is, its proponents admit they must change the very definition of science to include supernatural explanations.
>
> Judge Jones said that teaching intelligent design as science in public school violated the First Amendment of the Constitution, which prohibits public officials from using their positions to impose or establish a particular religion.
>
> "To be sure, Darwin's theory of evolution is imperfect," Judge Jones wrote. "However, the fact that a scientific theory cannot yet render an explanation on every point should not be used as a pretext to thrust an untestable alternative hypothesis grounded in religion into the science classroom or to misrepresent well-established scientific propositions."[16]

But the Jones ruling, though forthright and sensible, does not cut quite to the bone. At bottom, intelligent design seems to me like a regime-based effort to dumb down the American electorate to the point where said electorate will be chronically susceptible to Republican rhetoric and subject to Republican power.

These are all mass-market effects. They all reflect an economic reality in which professional standards have dissolved into apathy and cynicism, and the long-term building of a literate and critical public is rejected in favor of political power or quarterly returns. As mass-marketers cater to ignorance, presume ignorance, and prolong ignorance, so they vulgarize their constituencies. This creates a vicious cycle in which many citizens become too culturally enervated to judge quality or demand it.

Conclusion. The rule of vulgarity in America is far from complete. The *New York Review of Books,* the *New York Times,* the *New Yorker* (in its finer hours), and a variety of other periodicals, predictable lapses notwithstanding, maintain their commitment to consciousness. The same may be said for NPR and PBS. College campuses retain miscellaneous pockets of real learnedness, and a few, like St. John's (Annapolis and Santa Fe), Swarthmore (Pennsylvania), and Reed (Portland, Oregon), actually demand intellectual growth from their students. History departments, recent scandals notwithstanding, remain bastions of academic professionalism. And some corporations have gotten the idea that leading customers down the road to perdition may not be the most promising long-term strategy available.

Noteworthy as well is the American sense of humor, which continues to hack away at mass-market grossness. Jon Stewart, Stephen Colbert, and Bill Maher brighten the airwaves; *The Simpsons* has taken up the standard left behind by *All in the Family* at the forefront of the Vulgarity Patrol; and from Hollywood, a frequent offender, there is the occasional glimmer of hope from David Mamet, Eddie Murphy, the Coen brothers, and others. Unfortunately, however, American vulgarity is not just a laughing matter. Nor will turning away in disgust make things any better. Nationally, vulgarity is the major source of economic, physiological, and spiritual waste. Its faces may vary, but at heart it is the same: a goose of ignorance, kept fat by a mass market. And its grip on large numbers of Americans cannot be eased until we face it for what it is.

CHAPTER TWO

WASTE AND WISDOM

I casually asked him, "What is vulgarity?" merely to see what he would say, not supposing it possible to get a sudden answer. He thought for about a minute, then answered quietly, "It is merely one of the forms of Death."   John Ruskin, *Modern Painters*

Vulgarity and the Demographics of Waste

In the economics of the human spirit, every activity creates some sort of product: Sleep produces refreshment, stress produces fatigue, study produces skills, and so on. The results of some actions are positive, while others result in loss. Considering American vulgarity along these lines, we find that its product is waste: a waste that is not only economic and tangible but also cultural and intellectual.

The Dollar Impact. In 2002, a court awarded a single American smoker $28 billion in damages to be paid by the tobacco company that, in the court's judgment, had been responsible for the plaintiff's cancer. The sum was eventually reduced to $28 million, but even at that more reasonable figure, payment for the 170,000 new cases of lung cancer that are diagnosed *every year* would amount to $4.76 trillion, or roughly the size of the national debt.[17] Though settlements on this scale are not feasible, a Justice Department prosecution team led by Sharon Eubanks won a major lawsuit against Big Tobacco, with a recommended penalty of $130 billion. When the court reduced the penalty to $10 billion, Eubanks resigned, characterizing her superiors as "political appointees." As of early 2006, the Justice Department is investigating the case.[18]

Lawsuits based on similar principles have been mounted against fast-food marketers. Fast-food regulars tend to be overweight, putting themselves at risk for heart disease and diabetes, respectively America's first and sixth chief cause of death. The lawsuits refer to a corporate practice I mentioned earlier: the deliberate manipulation of ingredients in order to encourage overeating. The U.S. government, which has seen health-care expenses skyrocket, is considering new regulations on such foods and practices. Medical issues relating to overweight already rival tobacco-related illness in terms of economic impact.[19]

After these huge, and growing, liabilities of vulgarity, there are a few more dollar expenses to be tallied. What are the costs of gambling and other legalized addictions to addicts and their families? How much of the expense caused by violent crime can be attributed to gambling and addiction, to the media that market violence, and to the weapons market? What is the cost when a large percentage of Americans, poorly educated and poorly informed about their choices in life, is besieged by marketers hawking the quick fix?

The Cost in Human Capital. Vulgarity creates its own slum, even in the mansions of the mighty. The vulgar life is lived in fits and starts, from smoking break to smoking break, from meal to meal. The mass market and its hostages are enemy to time and phobic to reflection. The big picture of real events, with its implications of personal development, is occluded by the distractions and exhaustion of the short term. One fix necessitates another: aspirin for the hangover, antacid for the effects of lunch, coffee to get the energy up, and a smoke to take the edge off the upper. As we deal with these momentous matters, our lives slip by.

We figure the human cost of this life, not in damages, but in terms of the value that might have been created under more decent circumstances. This is *potentially* a dollar value if we consider the rise in the GNP that would occur if the market in vulgarity were dismantled by educated and well-informed consumers. But it is more importantly an unquantifiable human value, in that an intelligent and well-informed populace is itself an investment in the future of humanity.

Can all these wasteful activities be remedied, or are they simply a part of America's way of life? Things can be changed, I would answer, but things never change for the better until people become aware of wasteful practices and realize that they, as people, can make a difference. Change can be achieved in two ways: regulation and a wiser marketplace.

Solution A: The Four Types of Regulation

For several years during the late 1990s, I drove a 1979 Oldsmobile Toronado, a hulking coupe with a muscular V-8 and an engine compartment big enough to climb into. The first time I changed a tire, the car taught me a lesson. As I took off the wheel, I caught sight of the disk brakes. They were the biggest I'd ever seen on a passenger car.

The lesson I learned was that as systems grow bigger and more powerful, they need more and more regulation. This regulation can be technical (the brakes, the accelerator, the steering wheel), cybernetic (the driver), or social (the traffic laws, the police, the courts). Good drivers who obey reasonable laws are de facto self-regulating entities immune to regulation from the police or the courts. Thus, in systems large and small, self-regulation forestalls regulation from outside. Call this the Toronado Principle.

Since that day, I've applied this principle, often with helpful results, to every system I've looked at, from an insect's body to the United Nations. It works with both positive and negative examples:

POSITIVE: The American founding fathers equip their new republic with checks and balances by creating three branches of government —executive, legislative, and judicial—that balance each other and engage with each other. This government, by and large, governs and regulates not only the people but also itself.

NEGATIVE: Microsoft, on its way to becoming the world's biggest corporation, fails to establish an internal office to track corporate policy with reference to antitrust legislation. For want of this self-governance, Microsoft is sued by the Justice Department and must consign its fate to the hands of federal judges.[20]

The Toronado Principle offers a simple but eloquent message: *Regulate thyself, or thou shalt get regulated by somebody else.*

It is amazing how often, in the Land of the Free, this message goes unheard. Many economists and executives hold, as apparently Microsoft did, to the Adam Smithian theory that markets regulate themselves without any self-scrutiny or external oversight. But this theory, so brash and bold, turns out to be a fairyland myth. Free markets can never operate on a national scale, and in fact they have never been tried. That is because every nation has lawyers, courtrooms, and judges. The free market, as we know it, is actually a market regulated by litigation. Litigation is famously confrontational, crude, time-consuming, and expensive. "Free market" economics may look elegant in theory, but in practice it is clumsy and wasteful—something like touch parking.

This exhausts two types of regulation. Free-market theory is apparently a nonstarter, and regulation by lawsuit is unattractive. A third alternative is government regulation, usually involving agencies with three-letter acronyms: FDA, FTC, SEC, FAA, FCC. These regulators are costly, fallible, and time-consuming. Yet they remain in place because of a consensual perception that, without them, "chaos will come again." One of the greatest advantages of federal regulation is that it regularly, if sometimes belatedly, brings dangerous practices to public notice. The administrators of these agencies are appointed, rather than elected, and so are immune to the lure of campaign contributions. But they are not beyond the bias of their appointers or the web of quid pro quo transactions that is business as usual in Washington. The George W. Bush administration, for example, has tried to transmogrify at least two agencies—the Justice Department and the Federal Communications Commission (FCC)—from judicious watchdogs into weapons of political interest.[21] Redress for tactics of this sort requires congressional oversight. Federal regulation, in other words, is a mixed bag.

There is, finally, what might be called collegial regulation: regulation by independent, professional authorities, like bar associations for lawyers or medical associations for doctors. This sort of regulation has the twin advantages of being independent of government and conversant with the industry it governs. Collegial regulation works exceptionally well in law and medicine, whose professionals are under license and may lose their licenses if their practices cause harm. But such regulators would not be nearly as effective in the Microsoft case or the information industry at large, where licensing is not required. Nonetheless, collegial regulation would be preferable to lawsuits, if something like it could be instituted in the general marketplace.

Solution B: A Wiser Marketplace

More effective and sustainable than any external form of regulation is the creation of a wiser marketplace. But here wisdom must be born, not of training, but of painfully slow dialectical stress.

To understand this process, consider how the four conventional forms of regulation can work in the case of fast foods and overweight. Look back at the spring of 2003. Big Macs and Whoppers still reign supreme—a example of the "free market" in full career and compelling evidence of America's addiction to the chemicals that these foods deliver. But opposition springs up from another free-market player, the journal *Health Affairs,* in which an article coauthored by Eric Finkelstein reports that obese patients are costing the U.S. government tens of billions of dollars annually. On May 15, 2003, Finkelstein is interviewed on NPR—itself a hybrid free-market player. Should the obese be taxed higher than the non-obese for their medical care? What role in general should the federal government play? Anti-fast-food advocate John Banzhaf of George Washington University has already been more specific:

For example, my law students instigated a class action law suit against McDonald's, charging that it misrepresented the contents of its famous french fries. As the *Chicago Tribune* reported, the suit has already forced McDonald's to apologize for "duping" people, and noted that "even the most careful consumers can't protect themselves when a food producer hides what's in its product."[22]

Banzhaf, a law professor who once spearheaded the anti-tobacco movement, declares that he would prefer government regulation to lawsuits. This regulation would necessarily involve the Food and Drug Administration (FDA), but the FDA is chronically slow to act. On the other hand, a collegial regulator, the American Medical Association, is on the warpath against fast foods and obesity.[23]

A medical Tower of Babel? Unquestionably, there is a family resemblance, but it is exactly through cacophonous interactions of this sort that real history slowly develops. It was this way with cigarette smoking thirty years ago. Increasing public knowledge will erode the fast-food position. Lawsuits will be filed, especially when it can be shown that fast-food marketing misrepresented the nutritional content of its products or conspired to use chemicals in a quasi-addictive strategy. Moved at last by these events, the FDA will require health warnings on high-fat dishes and then, if necessary, regulate the food content. The fast-food industry, sensing that evolving public opinion has created a rich new market, will work to make healthy dishes sinfully delicious. Corporations will adopt new health policies. Consumer tastes will refine themselves. The marketplace will wise up.[24]

It has not escaped my notice that this analysis suggests a free-market position in modified form. After all, has not an interaction of individual forces produced a renewal in economics? Isn't the market choosing for itself? Yes, but only if we understand *market* to mean the full complement of real players: consumers, producers, lawyers, the press, advocacy groups, watchdog groups, collegial regulators, and even government itself. Because all these players are economically affected by the character of what is bought and sold, and because all of them form and participate in a huge information network that generates the character of economic interaction, all these players must be included in our idea of the market.[25]

The market is everybody, including the Feds. Call that the Second Toronado Principle.

The two Toronado principles and the example of fast foods suggest the enormous preferability of self-regulation and collegial regulation to litigation or federal regulation. Do the right thing for your customers, keep their interests at heart, and you will stay away from the hospitals, the courts, the Feds, and Chapter Eleven. Doing so will not mean that you have to go small and funky. Subway, Inc., has taken a reasonable food concept and made a mint with it. In a more exalted culinary realm, the Berkeley, California, restaurant Chez Panisse, brainchild of Alice Waters, has made its mark on high-end American cuisine with a menu rich in healthy vegetables. Its mission statement emphasizes health and conservation:

> Chez Panisse gathers its material from known and trusted purveyors, known to be committed themselves to sound and sustainable practices, and trusted to remain informed and responsive to these values in a rapidly changing society.
>
> By soundness we mean healthful products and practices, as pure and natural as possible, without synthetic additives or pollutants, without unnecessary complexities of packaging and marketing. By sustainability we mean conservation of resources, both natural resources like the families, businesses, and networks that plant and harvest and provide.[26]

This commitment has not involved an economic sacrifice but rather has rocketed Chez Panisse to the top of the heap among American restaurants (it was named Best Restaurant in America by *Gourmet Magazine* in 2001), and Waters has gone on to take her ideas about good food, sustainability, and healthy produce into cookbooks and schools.

The Chez Panisse phenomenon holds a surprising message, not only about food, but also about the nature of markets in general.

Alice Waters did not set out to found a health foods restaurant, but it turned out that healthy foods tasted better than the alternatives, and she ran with the idea. As time passed, this idea became a message reverberating with innovative chefs everywhere and even inspired a new mode of education. Can this sort of revolution happen in fast foods? Conceivably it can, if the addicting manipulation of sugars and fats is taken out of the equation. If we can do this, we can provide a level playing field and a much freer market. In any case, the Chez Panisse story suggests that American markets can indeed wise up and that the most energetic and sustainable reform of industry can come from within industry itself.

Fast foods, or at least their fat-soaked majority, have harmed their clients in four ways: esthetically, by turning an event that should be enjoyed at leisure into a gastronomic sprint; physiologically, by laying the foundation for heart disease and diabetes; economically, by condemning their victims (and other taxpayers) to decades of higher health-care costs; and intellectually, by depriving their customers of essential truths about the food they eat. Thus fast foods are a classic case of vulgarization: the fine art of turning a profit via the diminishment of public taste, public health, public wealth, and public consciousness. But the fast-food phenomenon has also shown us how an information-hungry society responds, slowly but massively, to a perceived injustice. There is no quick cure for market-induced vulgarity. But when cures develop, via improved information and education, they are not soon forgotten.

CHAPTER THREE

POLITE VULGARITY: AMERICAN COMPLACENCY AND ITS SUPPLIERS

Complacency in Action

In January 1993, President Bill Clinton took residence in the White House to lead a nation relieved by the end of the Cold War but concerned about domestic affairs. Clinton's choices for his key cabinet positions, though they did not raise many hackles at the time, might give some pause to a historian reading the roster with a few years of hindsight. For secretary of state, Warren Christopher, a statesman of professional standing but little personal presence. For secretary of defense, Les Aspin, a congressman with no experience in leadership or command. For secretary of the treasury, Lloyd Bentsen, a solid citizen but no past master of federal financial strategies. For secretary of commerce, Ron Brown, a politico better known for slick inside-the-Beltway interactions than for achievements in the realm of commerce. And for attorney general, Janet Reno, a woman completely inexperienced (as were the Clintons themselves) in D.C. networking or the national arena.

Clinton's first programmatic strategies were equally bemusing. He hastily went after reform for gays in the military, only to discover that he had walked into a labyrinth of ingrained attitudes and ethical conundrums. Worse yet, he embarked on a mammoth reform in health care, giving the reins over to his wife, Hillary, who was expert neither in health care nor in the Byzantine ways of Capitol

Hill. Worst of all, these domestic distractions were accompanied by a dramatic weakening of America's international intelligence and a disconnect, wrought by Clinton appointee Louis Freeh, between the Federal Bureau of Investigation (FBI) and the Central Intelligence Agency (CIA).

None of these choices turned out well, for the Clintons or for the nation. By early 1996, the initial array was a shambles. Gay reform and health care had gone nowhere. Christopher and Bentsen had resigned. Brown and Reno were under fire. Les Aspin had ignorantly refused a request for reinforcements from a field commander, causing eighteen American deaths in Somalia; Aspin, too, resigned. Weakened U.S. intelligence could not keep up with international terrorism, and when Sudan offered the arch-terrorist Osama bin Laden to Clinton for trial in 1996, the president could not be troubled to accept him.[27] Bill Clinton would learn from his mistakes and substantially clean up his act, but in two terms, he never fully recovered from a calamitously shaky start.

How could a single man make so many mistakes, and why were they not uproariously decried by a disappointed and indignant people? A likely answer to both questions is that Clinton wanted things a bit too cozy, as did most of his fellow Americans. Unlike JFK, who went for the best and the brightest, Clinton went for a cabinet that he thought he could work with—people who, moreover, would not upstage his own big personality. Though Clinton liked achieving, he also liked being liked, a trait not always conformable with presidential achievement. Clinton had political debts to pay, and sometimes paid them with appointments. Clinton had beaten Bush the First partly by making ambitious campaign promises, but it turned out that, in many cases, he had not formulated effective plans to keep them. Clinton's biggest campaign promise may have been a secret promise, to his wife, that she would get a major role in government.[28] But most importantly, despite his rhetorical sheen of competence and consciousness, Clinton was inexperienced. His biggest venue had been Arkansas, a state whose total population was just under that of Chicago. And he compounded this disadvantage by surrounding himself with an inexperienced cabinet.

Vulgar? One might argue in the affirmative, but one does not have to, because any particular *bêtises* of Clinton's were dwarfed by the overarching vulgarity of the nation that elected and would reelect him. Clinton's campaign and election were symptomatic of a traditional American shortsightedness. When the Cold War ended, the United States promptly forgot the world, turning its attention to what had traditionally concerned it the most: its own wallets and its own bellies. Appropriately, it cast into the cold the thrice-tried George Bush in favor of a charming Southerner who spoke fluent Purse and Tummy. Clinton was reelected in 1996 partly for the same reasons, and partly because his Republican opponent, Senator Bob Dole, ran a timid and unimaginative campaign.

Then the party began. While Africa seethed and Afghanistan festered, Americans turned to their dot-coms and their dim sum. While Osama bin Laden fine-tuned his detonative skills in New York, Yemen, Saudi Arabia, and Egypt, Americans were into mutuals and microbrews. While the same bin Laden deconstructed the U.S. embassies in Kenya and Tanzania, lit professors in the States taught deconstruction and other theories that denied all objectivity and all value. And if you grew tired of being a deadbeat yourself, you could turn on the most popular sitcom of the decade: *Seinfeld,* a series that dealt, ad nauseam, with a group of deadbeats.

But such diversions were not enough. Americans needed some real action. And so, as Al Qaeda drew up its own list of exciting surprises, Americans headed to the box office to watch Clint Eastwood in *A Perfect World* and *In the Line of Fire,* Mel Gibson in *Conspiracy Theory* and *Lethal Weapon: 3* and *4,* and Arnold Schwarzenegger in *True Lies* and *Last Action Hero.* But even these thrilling movies, and the suspenseful novels of Stephen King, Anne Rice, John Grisham, and Michael Crichton, the wonders of television, and the adrenaline rush of extreme sports, were not enough for a growing number of Yanks. Americans in greater and greater number complained to their doctors about depression. Many people expressed the sense that they were not finding enough meaning in life. These complainers were duly medicated. Drug sales soared.

This emotional muddle, this disregard for the important in favor of the trivial, this typically American deflation of meaning and attention, reached its climax in early 1998, when the press learned of President Clinton's erotic relationship with a White House intern. For many weeks, world news was hung out to dry in favor of one of the most banal, most predictable, and least disturbing of interactions: a young woman's fling with a middle-aged power monger. The press's inflation of the encounter at first might seem pure folly, but in fact it was something worse: The media knew that they could do a land office business in American vulgarity. True, the affair might be of no real importance at all, but oral sex in the Oval Office was just the sort of thing that the American public would lap up.

Not to be outdone by the media in terms of blatant vulgarity, congressional Republicans tried to stir up the worst sort of trouble possible—impeachment—from the ashes of the president's embarrassment. Their case, which rested on a relatively minor offense, was incurably weak, so weak that it never should have been tried, but the impeachment fiasco further diverted America's attention away from the world that it was supposed to be leading, and towards the besotted fads, ignorant delights, and petty squabbling that Americans had come to be so well known for. Even Europeans long acquainted with our simple ways were surprised at the flap. They shook their heads, uncertain whether a nation that freaked out over half-baked adultery would ever be literate in the ways of the world.

What Europeans gaped at as naive and stupid could be more clinically characterized as complacent. Complacency is the attitude that ignores problems, even whole sectors of problems, on the pretext that they are comparatively minor and will go away. Averting their gaze from these areas, the complacent focus instead on themselves and their personal pains and pleasures. Complacent parents spoil their children rotten, robbing kids' lives of aspiration and structure. Complacent spouses take their mates' love for granted, in order to concentrate on their putting stroke or weight-loss plan; when their marriages break up, they fob it off as infidelity or incompatibility. The complacent ignore, to their own peril, the fact that human relationships demand survival skills like engagement, inquiry, love, and courage. These survival skills apply to politics as well.

Complacency is dangerous, then, but is it vulgar? You might say that complacency is polite vulgarity, a vulgarity practiced by people who are bright and affluent and well-spoken: a vulgarity of perspective.

Let us look at two examples of polite vulgarity as practiced by the American media.

On April 22, 2000, NPR canceled its planned coverage of Earth Day International to follow the federal raid on the Little Cuba (Miami) home of Elián González's great uncle Lazaro. This switch drew public attention away from what is arguably the most crucial concern of the new century, international environmental policy, to an event whose only real importance was that it revealed the marginal executive adequacy of Attorney General Janet Reno. Why did NPR do such a thing? Probably for two reasons, both commercial and both vulgar. The press corps had been building up the González case as a human interest story (*Who gets the Cute Little Boy?*). Miami was in America, while Earth Day International was, well, international. The upshot was that NPR uncharacteristically drew attention away from what was international and important to what was national and trivial.

During the afternoon of June 2, 2005, I check out the home page of Fox News. Of the fifteen featured headlines, all but two concern America or Americans. While these headlines include "Rare Nickel Sells for $4.15 M" and "$2 M Settlement in Girl's Marshmallow Death," they do not include the car-bomb murder of Samir Kassir, a prominent Lebanese journalist, and they ignore as well a major U.S. diplomatic initiative in the Middle East. Fox's emphases suggest that, in their opinion, America would rather grovel in its own base pursuits than engage itself in the fate of the world.

This message is nothing new. Similar things have been said of us by outsiders for centuries. And they will remain substantially true until we write new forms of consciousness into our culture.

The Roots of Complacency

Where is the capital of American Vulgar? Las Vegas takes a lot of heat for its grossness, as does Los Angeles. Select Midwestern cities are also cited, when the citers, usually foreigners, can remember the names. But a reasonable case could be made for it being somewhere in Texas.

Some time ago, I was driving through northern Texas on my way from New York to San Francisco. On the evening of the Fourth of July, I stopped at a local playing field to watch the town fire department set up its celebratory fireworks display. The playing field was about a mile north of town, and a fierce and torrid north wind was combing the grass. Just after dark, the festivities commenced. The rockets launched impressively enough, but no sooner were they off the ground than they hit the full force of the gale, which swept them out of sight towards town. Undeterred by these threatening auspices, the firemen went on with their task, as though secure in the knowledge that good things happen to people who do their jobs well. Soon we all heard distant explosions and sirens. The firefighters leapt into their trucks and raced off in the direction of the town that they had set ablaze.

A book by Anne McDonald Maier describes another Texan enormity:

> The bizarre case of Wanda Holloway, arrested and tried in 1991 for soliciting the murder of Verna Heath, mother of her daughter's [Channelview, Texas] junior-high-school cheerleading rival, is detailed by a *People* magazine staffer and lawyer. Maier explains that cheerleading is so important in Texas because high school

football is such a major preoccupation there; she also tells of Holloway's teenage ambition, frustrated by her puritanical father, to be a pompom girl. While she [Holloway] pushed her daughter Shanna to be what she [Holloway] had been denied, Heath was also promoting her [own] daughter Amber to be a cheerleader. Although the two women had been friends before Amber began beating out Shanna, Holloway wanted Amber's mother dead so that Amber could not compete. When Holloway asked her ex-brother-in-law to hire a hit man to kill Heath, he took her request to the police.[29]

This one was too good for just a book. It became a Holly Hunter movie, entitled *The Positively True Adventures of the Alleged Texas Cheerleader-Murdering Mom* (1993).

With the idea of a mother trying to murder another mother, or even being accused of same, on the issue of which daughter made the junior high school cheerleading team, we may well have reached the Heart of Darkness, the inner sanctum of American Vulgar. Many of the elements of Americana are here—the small town, the school athletics, the competitiveness, the exuberance, the pubescent performers, the ogling audience—but they are overshadowed by mind-boggling complacency, the blind ignorance, the threat of fatal violence, and a gaping void of perspective. Additionally, the story reflects two other elements of textbook American vulgarity: the use of violence against athletic rivals (viz, Tonya Harding against Nancy Kerrigan, Detroit, 1994) and the premature display of a young girl's charms to male audiences (the murdered tot-beauty-queen JonBenet Ramsey, Boulder, Colorado, 1997). All these elements working together make the Channelview case the real McCoy, the locus classicus of a culture known for creating, maintaining, rewarding, and honoring ignorance.

Texas' prominence on the landscape of American Vulgar is due primarily to its location and its geology. Texas is huge (larger than France) and isolated. Its main population centers, Houston, San Antonio, and Dallas/Fort Worth, lie far from cities of comparable size and relatively far from each other. Its large population and strong economy owe themselves to oil, the drilling of which has produced such exorbitant wealth that a fortune of $100 million is casually referred to as a "unit." Because of these circumstances, Texan marketers have adopted the idiom of size, selling their state in terms of bigger skies, bigger houses, bigger meals, bigger sex, and bigger bathrooms. Thus, Texas has become the flagship of a big nation, whose culture is known internationally for its assumption that Bigger Is Better.

Isolation in space can also mean isolation in time: disconnection from the facts and judgments of history. San Antonio proudly displays the most famous ruin in America, the Alamo, as a fort in which a small force of brave fighters held out to the last man against a superior force of heartless Mexicans. A number of Hollywood films honor this view of history. Texas-on-line.com (a private company) offers the following narrative of the events leading up to the war:

> The colonization of Texas as a Mexican state brought Anglos westward from the United States and Mexicans northward. Differences in language and culture led to tension. Most Mexicans were Catholic and most Anglos were Protestant. The Americans felt ties to the United States, not Mexico. Trade grew between Texas and the United States, alarming Mexico. In 1830, the Mexican Congress passed a law that stopped American immigration into Texas. It initiated custom collections as the government tried to stay in control. Dissatisfaction spread among the settlers, and in 1832, skirmishes broke out that signaled the coming revolution.

But, as historian Quintard Taylor explains, bans on immigration and new customs collection were far from the most prominent reasons for the war:

> By 1835 Texas slaveholders had duplicated the U.S. Slave system. Fully 10 percent of English-speaking Texans were slaves. Slaveholders now demanded protection of their property and open commerce in human beings. Texas and Mexico were on a collision course.

African Americans, free and slave, would soon be caught in the middle of these contesting sides. For many Texas slaves Mexico's flag represented liberty.[30]

Mexico was fighting to free the slaves, while the Texans were fighting to keep them. Texas is in fact the only region of America to have seen *two* wars fought in support of slavery. The glorification of the Alamo, and the necessary suppression of history for this glorification, exemplify the way in which public discourse can vulgarize its audience by denying them the facts.

It is from geographical roots of this kind, from states like isolated nations, from small-town and even urban cultures cut off from any international or national continuity of values, that American complacency springs. And this complacency, this simple neglect of what the world is generating around us, reaches out to encircle what we learn, what we buy, and whom we elect.

Gullibility and How We Achieve It. Complacency and obliviousness are cognate with gullibility. Americans who would rather not be bothered about international affairs will believe virtually anything that flatters their ignorance. For this reason Americans, for all their universities, foundations, and think tanks, have long been regarded by their international neighbors as informationally challenged. The series of informational disconnects, neglected warnings, unnoticed clues, heedless decisions, and botched assignments that led up to the U.S. intelligence disaster of 9/11 was, we hope, the crowning embarrassment in a long history of faux pas. Here is the investigative reporter Seymour Hersh quoting a Pentagon critique of America's informational eagle, the CIA:

> The agency's [CIA's] analysts . . . "were generally reluctant throughout the Cold War to believe that they could be deceived about any critical question by the Soviet Union or other Communist states. History has shown this view to have been extremely naive." [The Pentagon officials] suggested that political philosophy, with its emphasis on the variety of regimes, could provide an antidote to the C.I.A.'s failings, and . . . "alerts one to the possibility that

political life may be closely linked to deception. Indeed, it suggests that deception is the norm in political life, and the hope, to say nothing of the expectation, of establishing a politics that can dispense with it is the exception."[31]

In the greater context of Hersh's article, this passage is doubly ironic. First, according to Pentagon officials, the CIA, an agency assigned specifically to gathering, analyzing, and evaluating information, was seriously and continuously duped by the Communists, even though the agency took the Communists to be Cold War enemies.

Second, Hersh presents the Pentagon view that "political life may be closely linked to deception" as though it were some new insight, when in fact it is a saw as old as politics itself. To ancient wisdom, even the gods were deceivers, and the two most famous mortal deceivers, Odysseus and Jacob, were especially blessed by divinity. Theoretically, the linkage between politics and deception dates backed to Protagoras (fifth century BC), who held that, in the absence of demonstrable truth, the best political instrument is a convincing tongue. Is Hersh, the Investigator of Investigators, himself a victim of our national provinciality? In America, stranger things have happened.

Why are Americans so easily deceived? Complacency, as I averred earlier, is one reason. But other factors are equally worthy of attention.

As our world grows more technical and more complicated, we put more and more faith in specialists: consultants, accountants, doctors, lawyers, legislators, the media, and so on. And as we rely more and more on specialists, our personal worlds, with their sense of autonomy and responsibility, diminish proportionally. In short, the increasing reliance on specialized services amounts to the deterioration of personal knowledge and the slow demise of the public self. Moreover, as the special fields that we depend on grow more complicated, we are more and more likely to accept wholesale, rather than to analyze or question, the information that our specialists offer us. One danger of this imposed credulity is exemplified by the Establishment rationale for invading Iraq. The Bush administration informed the public that war was justified because Iraq had weapons of mass destruction. This statement was deceptive in that it was not supported by any solid evidence and in that it omitted other major reasons for going to war. But it was initially believed, both by the majority of the public and by the armed forces. We want to believe in our experts for the simple reason that, so often, we *have* to believe in them. But our reliance on them increases our gullibility.

Moreover, we are educated to be gullible. Of the tens of thousands of administrators now trying to fine-tune our high school and college curricula, precious few are interested in the kind of individual, the kind of citizen, that education creates. Instead, attention is devoted to balancing the demands of competing disciplines and, when possible, to the development of marketable skills. The idea that the bachelor's degree should include, as a requirement, historical perspective and critical thinking is generally out of fashion and, in many venues, has never been tried. And, to the extent that historical perspective and critical thinking are lacking, our graduates lack the mental instrumentation to evaluate the information that they receive. They are fully certified degree holders in Credulity. More on this in Chapter 8.

Finally, Americans are gullible because they are information starved. Here, the smoking gun lies right at the door of the Press Club. Journalists are quick to parrot the official version of political reality or to spice things up with the latest celebrity rape. But the real interesting stuff—the news that might challenge authority—is regularly suppressed. Ohio, the swing state in the 2004 presidential election, was riddled with voting fraud introduced by the state's Republican power structure, but somehow this did not make much news.[32] The now-notorious "K Street Project," a quid pro quo conspiracy in which Republican congressmen actually lobbied corporations to hire Republican lobbyists, who would in turn lobby *them*, flew under the radar until the Jack Abramoff scandal of 2005–2006 blew the lid off. And when, in early 2006, it became clear that Supreme Court nominee Samuel Alito, together with the president and top members of his administration, subscribed to the "unitary executive theory" originated by pro-Nazi extremist Carl Schmitt, no major news source jumped on the story.[33] Apparently, it now takes high-visibility indictments, rather than merely alarming news, to capture the attention of the American press corps. Without such attention, the American electorate is at once more ignorant of the truth and more apt to believe the lies that it is told. More on this in Chapter 10.

Complacency and Depression. I hinted earlier that complacency was related to depression. Here are my reasons for making that connection.

Although the word *complacent* suggests pleasure (coming from the Latin for "to please"), the complacent usually are not happy people. If happiness is indeed the process of engagement in life, and dialogue with life, that most psychologists describe, then it is not bestowed on people who compulsively wall themselves off from potentially painful topics and interactions. You could actually call depression the Bartleby Syndrome, after Herman Melville's fictional scribe who worked on Wall Street and whose office window opened onto a brick wall. Bartleby's fatal depression is continually linked to his walling himself away from the continuum (as in his slogan "I would prefer not to"). Complacency is little more than a dressed-up version of *denial,* a syndrome characteristically linked to depression.[34]

It may seem curious that the mere avoidance of pain and danger, which in itself would seem to be a survival instinct, can so regularly leave us depressed. But perhaps an even more profound instinct is at work. The ability to endure pain and danger in the name of something higher, and to integrate this endurance into our characters and our personal narratives, elevates us above physical survival and onto the level of spiritual survival and social evolution. Merely physical survivors are subject to all the internal and external punishments that nonachievement merits. Spiritual survivors, on the other hand, are invested in life and eligible for its pleasures.

With all these factors in mind, let us return to 1992, the year of Bill Clinton's first candidacy for the presidency of the United States. Suppose that Mr. Clinton had had a crystal ball and foreseen, event by event, the consequences of national complacency. Emerging from his prophetic meditation, he might have composed a rousing campaign speech to the effect that, the collapse of the U.S.S.R. and the victory over Iraq notwithstanding, America was still in a state of war. This state of war, he could have explained, would continue until tensions in the Middle East were resolved, until terror ceased to be a weapon of choice for factions and nations, until the purveyors of world energy came out of the Middle Ages, until vulgarity and its marketers were banished, and until American education was retooled to produce a conscious and effective citizenry. Only then, he might have said, could we declare a peace—but a peace that would have to be won again, a day at a time.

If Clinton had foreseen the future and spoken thus, he would have been telling the truth. But he sure wouldn't have gotten himself elected in *these* United States.

CHAPTER FOUR

VULGARITY, INC.; VULGARITY.COM

Vulgarity, Inc.

The public corruption is the foundation on which corporations always depend for their political power. There is a natural tendency to coalition between them and the lowest strata of political intelligence and morality; for their agents must obey, not question. They exact success, and do not cultivate political morality. The lobby is their home, and the lobby thrives as political virtue decays.

C. F. Adams, Jr., "A Chapter of Erie," in *Chapters of Erie* (1869)

Corporate vulgarity arises in several major forms and from several causes. In this chapter, I will try to give an example of each.

Information Slavery. In 1993, I attended a seminar that included a senior executive from one of America's top insurance companies. I happened to tell him that I sometimes wrote articles for another major insurer, in an in-house magazine that dealt with quality-of-life issues. He replied, with an air of seasoned wisdom and solid experience, that he could think of no reason why an insurance company should try to educate its clients.

Remind you of anybody? Distrust of communication is characteristic of executives. Some withhold information in the belief that this strategy will empower them (see "Conservation of Power," below). Some have no conception of the positive influence of lucidly conveyed information. Some are so congenitally secretive that they are phobic to talk and writing (it was said of a West Coast department head that "He kept secrets even from himself"). Most importantly, some—I fear more than some—are unable to handle information in the first place. They have reached their top positions by making sales or cutting deals or motivating staff, but nowhere along the line have they picked up legitimate analytic skills. When a considered decision is necessary, they rely on guesswork and impulse, and then dream up a plausible rationale.

Information deprivation can lead to information slavery, the world's most common form of bondage. Firms, foundations, and agencies ruled by self-absorbed and secretive executives can become information ghettos, where rumor is lord and distrust is universal. Business is weakened in two ways: first, because the staff lacks the tools necessary for the job, and second, because they lack the excitement of conscious autonomy. They have been vulgarized, forced into a position in which it is necessary to fudge reports, and convenient to lie to customers.

Information slavery has one further consequence: negation. Employees out of the flow of information are always saying no to things: to requests for special services, to requests for clarification, to questions about future products or policies. If they cannot find a product on the shelf, they will tell you it's no longer available or that it never even existed. If they have not heard of a new corporate service, they will tell you it simply isn't done. These depressed employees would rather invoke the power of negation than admit their own helpless ignorance of what is going on.

Conservation of Power. A Midwest corporate founder once confided to me the secret of his success. "I hired the dullest people I could," he said, "because I needed full control." This radical strategy worked for the first couple of years, but proved self-defeating in the long term. As the firm's business increased, more and more responsibility fell to the original staffers, who proved unequal to the task. The founder's successor continued his original policy of nondisclosure, with disastrous results. Founder and successor neglected a principle that operates both in nature and in society: that the total health or power of an individual or group must be measured *collectively* rather than in terms of a single dominant individual. For this reason alone, governments like that of North Korea, which tyrannizes its people, will never compete economically with governments like that of the United Kingdom, which prizes and preserves its citizens' freedom. The conservation of power degrades all participants and ultimately diminishes itself.

Conservation of power is of course coterminous with information slavery and seldom occurs without it. The upshot of both is a degeneration so communal that the system begins grinding to a halt. This unintentional slowdown provokes even more autocratic behavior from the front office, and a vicious cycle kicks in. Such dynamics are documented in David Mamet's acerbic if hamhanded play and movie, *Glengarry, Glen Ross* (film, 1992). Here a team of jaded urban realtors (in the film, Al Pacino, Jack Lemmon, Ed Harris, Alan Arkin) are warned by their bosses to produce or get out. Simultaneously, they are denied the information they need (leads about prospective buyers). These vicious-cycle tactics fail to improve business, instead producing paralysis, vituperation, and crime. The vulgarizing effects of top-down management are evident in the film's automatic profanity and ubiquitous depression.

Corporate Coma. Recently, I spent half an hour on the phone in vain. I called the family lawyer, but he was in a meeting. I tried an acquaintance in the state senate, but she was in caucus. I dialed up my publisher, but he was chairing a meeting. Just for relief, I phoned an old friend from the University of Oregon, but he was in committee. Finally, I attempted reaching my literary agent. He was in a meeting, his assistant told me, and it looked as though he'd never get out. Could I get him to call me next week? He'll be away all next week, she said. Where? At a conference.

What is everybody doing in these meetings, committees, and caucuses? They are doing the three things that American executives do best: wasting time, avoiding responsibility, and neglecting business. When these execs get a chance, they will attend a conference, where these skills will be strengthened and refined by nationally ranking experts. These proclivities, however, have not escaped the notice of a few spoilsports. Sidney Taurel, CEO of Eli Lilly, regaled his colleagues in 2000 with an outspoken essay on leadership that recommended individual decision-making and buck-stopping as opposed to committee procedures. His message: Save time, take responsibility, do business.[35]

American colleges and universities are among those worst afflicted with this form of corporate coma. The outside world may wonder whether professors spend more time at teaching or research, when in fact their most-spent and worst-spent time is in committees and other meetings. Professors and their deans may tell you that all this gabbing is an essential part of faculty self-governance, but I am convinced that much of academic committee structure derives equally from mutual distrust (now much greater in the currently politicized and polarized academic setting) and from personal anxiety about decision-making. Thus, decisions that could be made quite adequately by a single person are conscientiously chewed over by fifteen. The upshot is that our professors are working much harder than they used to, but not to such good effect.

Vulgar Panic.

An unexpected rise in jobless claims unnerved Wall Street on Thursday, sending stocks sharply lower on worries the market's recent rally might have come too far, too fast. . . . Yahoo! earnings which met, but didn't beat, estimates also disappointed investors. . . . "Yahoo! didn't deliver significant upside and it's a huge momentum name, so you have some momentum taken out of the market," said Keith Keenan, vice president of institutional trading at Wall Street Access, a New York-based brokerage firm. "The bulls anticipated much higher numbers." *New York Times,* July 10, 2003

Panic is a familiar phenomenon with crowds and a common feature of vulgarity. Panic is in fact the flip side of complacency, and so it is not hard to find individuals who are politically complacent but who panic if their favorite stock has a bad day. Panic, moreover, is a corporate product. Multibillion-dollar funds, which sell large blocks of stock on a given day, produce the dramatic price swings that fuel panic. So does the press, when it overreports worrisome events to capitalize on their crisis value. A few years ago, the indexes took a steep dip when it was reported that, according to a survey, people were spending less time at their computers. The report neglected to mention that overall computer use was still very much on the rise, but this item went unnoticed in the frenzied sell-off. Within weeks, this minor panic was forgotten, and investors, lulled into complacency, were ready to panic again.

The Corporate Other. I wake up coughing. Though it is full morning, the air is dark around my bedroom windows, and large pieces of ash can be seen falling like black snow. The air carries the sweet stink of acres of burning cane. A disaster? No, only another routine day in the Hawaiian Cane and Sugar Company's agricultural program. Can you call the police or your senator? No, what HC&S is doing is completely legal.

The American corporation is a legal entity and an economic necessity, but it can also be seen as a kind of monstrous birth. I call it the corporate other, because it is neither public nor private, and because it often refuses to communicate with individuals. If it has lobbying money, it becomes a kind of state-within-a-state, throwing its weight around without review by voters or oversight by government. In Chapter 2, I discussed the ways in which corporate purveyors of vulgarity sooner or later come under regulation. There are also corporations that, though they do not market vulgarity, nonetheless commit vulgar acts. These vulgarities range from low-grade but repeated annoyances like traffic or noise to potentially life-threatening abuses. You can complain to these corporations, but then you would be violating a special rule of life, which goes, "Never discuss the Problem *with* the Problem." The same insouciance that created the abuse will characterize the response to your complaints.

Cane-field burning is a textbook case of corporate vulgarity. The Hawaiian Cane and Sugar Company regularly degrades the lives of anyone caught in the path of its dense smoke. The corporation's awareness of its own malfeasance is evidenced by the fact that it employs a man who personally telephones a list of smoke-sensitive residents before burns in their area. But HC&S is active on other fronts as well. It makes campaign donations, uses lobbyists, and, now and then, announces publicly that it is working on less toxic alternatives to burning cane. There can be no appeal to law. Agricultural burning is legal in Hawaii, though private citizens are not permitted to burn leaves, presumably because doing so would pollute the air.

The full impact of field burning on public policy can be seen in a somewhat more evolved dispute concerning grass burning by seed companies in the Willamette Valley of Oregon. Individual citizens and various groups and publications protested this practice as offensive to the public, environmentally harmful, and potentially dangerous. But to no avail. Legislators in Salem were so protective of agriculture that you can almost hear cowbells in the senate chamber. Then, on August 3, 1988, a few miles south of Albany, Oregon, smoke from a controlled burn billowed onto Interstate 5, sealing off visibility. Seven people died in a forty-car wreck. Lawsuits connected with this accident got Salem's attention, and field burning in Oregon was speedily reduced by new state regulations.

Apparently, corporate air pollution, protected by soft money and lobbies, is too serious a matter to yield to public reason. You have to produce the dead bodies.

Corporate Gluttony.

Over the protests of 750,000 viewers and readers, three appointees to the Federal Communications Commission last month voted to permit the takeover of America's local press, television and radio by a handful of mega-corporations. If allowed to stand, this surrender

to media giantism would concentrate the power to decide what we
read and see—in both entertainment and news—in the hands of
an ever-shrinking establishment elite.

William Safire, "Big Media's Silence," New York Times, June 26, 2003

Thanks to the advocacy of *New York Times* writer Stephen Labaton
and the bipartisan response by legislators, including Ted Stephens
of Alaska, this ruling was not allowed to stand. Here is a powerful
example of how corporate gluttony can reach to the highest levels
of government, and how much force is required to withstand this
greed. It is especially dramatic that here the culprit was a regulatory agency, the FCC, whose partisan appointees supported a
measure that would have all but annulled diversity in American
journalism.

Why have monopolistic practices become so common? One
reason is that today's globalized high-tech markets favor big companies over small. Amazon.com behaves so much like our local bookstore that our local bookstore is now empty and for rent. Another
reason is that today's emphasis on quarterly profit ("bottom-
lining") over long-term growth encourages companies to use highly
aggressive strategies towards their competition. Instead of realizing
that long-term growth in the global economy will provide wealth
for all, many corporations lean towards the pirate strategy of Take
All or Die.

Which brings us back to gluttony, greed, and vulgarity. Today's
emphasis on bottom-lining reminds us that vulgarity in each of its
manifestations involves a negative attitude towards time, a disregard for the continuum of past and future, in favor of some immediate satisfaction. These quick-fix gratifications are transitory,
unsatisfying, and ultimately destructive. Rather than contributing
to robust competition and sustainable growth, they depress people,
interrupt progress, and deaden markets.

Vulgarity.com

Recently, the following exchanges of e-mail occurred between two dot-coms and me:

Comment: No more pop-ups, please. You are slowing up my business and violating my space. RGrudin

Reply: Thank you for contacting Cheap Tickets. We apologize for the negative experience you've had with the pop-ups on CheapTickets.com. We understand not all of them are directly travel related but CheapTickets.com has selected ads which we believe will greatly benefit our customers. Be aware that we do appreciate your input and will consider your suggestions when making future decisions. For exceptional savings on discounted flights, lodging, rental cars, vacation packages, cruises, and more, visit www.cheaptickets.com today! Thanks for making Cheap Tickets your premier travel provider. Travel Professionals are available 24/7 at 1-888-922-8849.

Thanks,

The Cheap Tickets Team

The Best Kept Secret in Travel

www.cheaptickets.com

Comment: No more pop-ups, please. You are slowing up my business and violating my space. Robert Grudin

Reply: Dear Robert,

Thank you for contacting Orbitz. We're sorry if you feel overwhelmed by our pop-up advertisements. Those ads are distributed by a third party, so Orbitz does not have any control over where and when Internet users receive them. If you wish to disable pop-up ads, go to www.panicware.com/products.html and download "Pop Up Stopper Free Edition." It's free and will stop all pop-up advertising—not just Orbitz' ads. To view a list of other software programs that block pop-up, go to http://www.webattack.com/Freeware/misctools/fwpopblock.shtml. Robert, we value you as a customer and look forward to serving you again in the future.

Sincerely,
Roger
Orbitz Customer Service
www.Orbitz.com
Most Low Fares Made Easy

Most readers will be familiar with pop-ups (*pops*, for short) as disagreeable, alien intrusions into one's daily work online.[36] Some, like Orbitz or Cheap Tickets, can be dispatched with an exit-click; others dominate the screen for a fixed period; still others will not go away until you either accede to their demands or reboot your computer. Pops are intrusive, tasteless, and demeaning. Together with spam, they add significantly to the special kind of anxiety that is seen as an adjunct of computer use.

Notice the responses to my request. Roger's initially patronizing tone ("We're sorry if you feel overwhelmed") turns into a plea of innocence ("Those ads are distributed by a third party, so Orbitz does not have any control over where and when Internet users receive them")—as though the third party were not being paid by Orbitz to get into our faces. The Cheap Tickets Team, on the other hand, neither apologizes nor excuses itself. Instead, Cheap Tickets proclaims that its ads, invited or uninvited, will "greatly benefit" its customers—in ways, one assumes, so obvious that it does not need to explain them, or that I must be a ninny not to understand. Cheap Tickets implies that it is simply going about its legitimate business, which just happens to be making sure that we cannot freely go about our own. Uninvited and intrusive, pops exploit and vulgarize the computer–user interface.

Roger kindly referred me to a free antipops service. More on that later.

Many major firms are deeply ambivalent about using pops—so much so that at least one has simultaneously attacked them and used them, as Rachel Konrad describes:

> Toyota Motor executives are adamant about respecting their customers' privacy, and they say they won't alienate buyers with Web

monitoring and other controversial online marketing tactics. So they were understandably caught off guard when informed by a reporter that some visitors to Ford.com were greeted with a prominent pop-up ad offering to redirect them to Toyota.com, a practice that seemed clearly at odds with the company's stated opposition to aggressive online advertising.[37]

Equally manipulative and degrading is a strategy called adware: software, surreptitiously bundled with Internet downloads, that then alerts corporations to a consumer's personal tastes and habits. As Konrad notes, adware usually generates a blizzard of pops:

> Fearful of a backlash from privacy advocates, representatives at dozens of the nation's top advertisers refused to talk about adware or said they were unsure whether their companies used it. But consumers who have downloaded ad-supported software on the Internet will quickly notice pop-up ads from Travelocity, Priceline. com, Thrifty, United Airlines, American Express, Honda, Daimler-Chrysler and Toyota. Retail companies such as Lancome and L'Oreal are experimenting with the trend, as are technology heavyweights like Microsoft, Oracle, Sprint and Verizon.

Executives tend to refer to practices like spam, pops, and adware as "creative" or "aggressive," but more aptly descriptive terms are available. Simply put, the adware-pops strategy means that big business is cheating its way into your house, stealing valuable information from you, and using that information to harass you with unsolicited messages. And there is nothing to guarantee that big business is not selling your information to others who will do the same.

In the end, there is little difference between companies that play games with adware and pops (call it *badware*) and the Hawaiian Cane and Sugar Company, which regularly chokes its neighbors with smoke. In both cases, private space is being violated in the name of corporate profit. If either is the less vulgar, it is the sugar people, who at least do not spy on you.

One more form of Vulgarity.com deserves brief mention. It occurred in the 1990s, when Microsoft was trying to embarrass another corporation, and the poor user stepped into the line of fire. Do you remember having been in the midst of some momentous computer project, only to see a new window with something like

> This program has performed an illegal operation
> and will now shut down.

Were the Feds coming after you? What could you or your program have done wrong? Maybe nothing at all. It might just have been Microsoft's way of spoiling your fun with some non-Microsoft, but "Windows compatible," program you happened to be running. Microsoft's policy was to see to it that competing software packages did not run quite as smoothly as its own. You, of course, were not supposed to realize this, but rather to vent your shame and frustration by buying Microsoft software. An insidious scheme, and quite typical of its practitioner, whose methods during this period have been described as follows:

> These [Microsoft's] methods include a tight integration of applications into the operating system, the bundling of applications with Windows to force competing application vendors out of the market, the mandatory bundling of Windows with new computer equipment, *deliberate limitations in the compatibility of their own software with competing products,* contracts that prohibit third parties to do business with anyone but Microsoft, and retaliatory practices against non-cooperating vendors.[38]

Microsoft has substantially cleaned up its act since its innings with the Justice Department (1998–2001). Its Windows XP has achieved dependable compatibility, and the corporation now employs world-class experts to maintain a high quality of user interface.

Taming Thebeast.com. My wife, who is breaking in a new laptop that runs Windows XP, calls me over to her desk. An "instant message" has just popped up. It sits in the middle of the screen, looking important and official. It is from someone we don't know named Jennifer. It offers, to each and all of us, her social and erotic attention.

And, by the way, do we have a webcam? I sit down at the laptop, delete Jennifer's greeting, and go to the HELP menu. After five minutes of grappling with instructions that seem deliberately obscure, I disable Windows Messenger once and for all.

In so doing, I experience the saving grace of the Internet and the programs that service it. The Internet business may be full of ills, but it is also full of remedies, and this abundance of remedies suggests a growing dialogue between providers and users: a wiser and wiser market. It is fitting that these wise-market effects should be so prominent in what we now call the *knowledge business*. Of all forms of knowledge, none is more valuable than the self-knowledge that leads to self-regulation.

CHAPTER FIVE

VULGARITY
AND NATURE

The Issue of Growth

If someday you would like to observe a near-perfect fitness club, as well as a model for a robust economy, go for a walk in a virgin forest. You will notice that none of its animal citizens is overweight (unless stocking up for hibernation) and that they go about their business with an alertness and an engagement unmatched in human society. Hang around for a few years, and you will notice something else of equal importance: Change is slow. Diverse animal and plant populations have achieved balance with each other. The forest, though full of liveliness, is historically at rest.

Of course, to learn this natural wisdom firsthand, you have to *find* a virgin forest, and that can be difficult. As of 1996, 95 percent of America's virgin timber had been logged. Saving the last 5 percent has become the mission of an advocacy group called Save America's Forests, but as of early 2006, the Act to Save America's Forests was still stalled in Congress. Admittedly, there is broad support for the bill, but it flies in the face of an American prejudice as old as the American Frontier: the insistence on unimpeded growth. Americans, it would seem, always want to push the envelope, and in this case, the envelope is a finite and defenseless environment.

Growth is not just a cultural obsession. Growth has become a theoretical model for economists, executives, and even civil servants. The idea is that economic entities, be they towns or corporations, cannot remain robust unless they keep growing, and that this growth imperative has no chronological limit. The growth people are no amateurs, either. They can cite factors and crunch numbers. But what they cannot do, apparently, is confront the dangers implicit in their model and their imperative. They would do well to note the teaching of the forest. They would do well to remember that the most dramatic example of unimpeded growth in nature is cancer, which kills its host and, necessarily, itself. The most colossal and preposterous of all vulgarities would be a civilization that, in the course of its busy, growing ways, paved over its environment and destroyed its only source of sustenance.

In "real-estate-ese," *growth* translates into "development." *Development* is a talismanic word to civil servants, because (given the growth model) the tax income derived from development is the only way that they can project civil services into the future. Civil servants, in the main, have to ignore the long term. They are paid to make things work, and cannot do so without an ever-increasing pool of funds. Often, the only way to pay the piper is through the approval of large-scale building projects.

Development usually takes place gradually, like floodwaters in Venice. Sometimes, however, it is so dramatic as to provoke attention. Take the Centennial-Newhall phenomena in Southern California in 2003. National attention focused on Los Angeles County's approval proceedings for Centennial and Newhall Ranch (how's "Ranch" for a developer's euphemism?), two housing developments so vast that, were they located in Oregon instead of neighboring California, they would immediately rank among the state's ten largest cities. These developments would eat up about 12,000 acres (18.5 square miles) of grassland in the Antelope and Santa Clarita valleys. The demographic impact of these and other planned subdivisions would be substantial:

> Between the two tract towns—whose plans include shopping centers, industrial parks, schools and libraries—and several smaller subdivisions, there will be an influx of more than 200,000 people

in the region. And that's just the beginning, according to analysts who predict that the population in the Santa Clarita Valley region could more than triple in size by 2030, with Interstate 5 as its primary connection to the Los Angeles job base.[39]

The environmental impact would also be severe, even if viewed only from the practical angles of water use and air pollution. But other threats inhered. Los Angeles County (about 4,000 square miles in area) would lose its remaining grassland habitats. Mountainous land aside, the county would become wall-to-wall city and suburb.

This disturbing observation was brought up by one of the developers, but instead of voicing regret that nature was being destroyed, he showed disappointment that there would soon be no more land to build on:

> "We see this providing a great pipeline of homes," said Jon Jaffe, Western region president of Lennar, which developed Stevenson Ranch in the area.
>
> "We view this as a great strategic opportunity for us. Los Angeles County has tremendous population growth that is projected to continue. L.A. County is very constrained as far as entitled land— a lot of the land is developed and a lot of it is mountainous and undevelopable."[40]

Predictably, such developments and attitudes arouse controversy. The opposition may have the moral high ground, but it is often proven to be short on legal clout. Development is built into county planning. Governments think in terms of the quality of services rather than the quality of life. Development produces capital value and makes "economic" sense, as Matthew Jalbert admits:

> As long as it is affordable to commute long distances, to buy a large single-family home, and to irrigate a green grass lawn in the desert, people will do so. Developers will build it, and they [buyers] will come. As long as cities and older suburban areas are considered dangerous and crowded and their schools inadequate, developments such as the Antelope Valley will be generated and continue to degrade the vitality of society and the Earth as a whole.[41]

To this might be added, "As long as planners are invested in a monolithic and obsessive model of growth . . ."

Is there any escape from unregulated growth? Only, writes economist Richard Douthwaite, if we can recontextualize our basic idea of growth and capital:

> Another good thing to have come from the World Bank recently is Ismail Serageldin's work on the Four Capitals approach to sustainability. The Four Capitals are physical, human, social, and natural capital. The idea here is that we are living on the income from these capitals—the benefits we enjoy are their product—and therefore sustainability entails each generation passing on to the next a stock of these four capitals at least equivalent to that which it received from the previous generation.[42]

Reconceiving economics in terms of four capitals is "sustainable" because it figures the environment directly into the equation:

> The [World] Bank's mental model focuses on finance, and to the degree that it embraces development, is a growth model that seems to assume: a high degree of substitutability between the "four capitals", social development through economic growth, and intrinsically strong environmental resilience.[43]

It is somewhat easier to understand how this is going to work in undeveloped countries, where the World Bank can exert enlightened leadership, than it is to project the model into developed national economies. Will the four-capitals approach trickle down to local financing? Nonetheless, the idea has merit in that it transforms economics from a merely fiscal study into an understanding of the humanity–nature continuum.

Let us look at how the four-capitals strategy might work in a small city (population 100,000–200,000) that desires economic growth without necessarily increasing its size. The city could increase its human capital by investing in primary and secondary education, starting a lifelong learning program, and rezoning an industrial area to accommodate a college campus. It could increase its natural capital with tough pollution laws, a light rail system, and parks that at once preserve nature and bring the natural world into the social infrastructure. The city could increase its social capital by creating programs in health education and focusing on law enforcement as a protective rather than punitive institution. And the city's physical capital—its money, that is—would grow, as a more highly skilled, healthier, and safer population evolves.

The economics of this projection is fairly simple. Because our population is skilled, it produces more money. Because it is enlightened, it loses less money to illness and crime.

The model of unlimited economic growth may be considered from four other perspectives: ethics, culture, natural curbs, and climax economics.

Ethics. Because stockholders and stock traders are hooked on "growth," the growth model often becomes an ethically corrupting force. Merely consider the dozens of book-cooking scandals of 2001–2002, the resultant bankruptcies, and the $1 trillion dip on Wall Street, and you get some idea of the danger of subscribing to the growth model. No matter how vehemently this model is defended, it simply does not account for the complex ebb and flow of economic reality. In other areas, its influence can border on the obscene. A federal investigation of the Redding Medical Center (Redding, California) and Tenet Healthcare, its parent, resulted in charges that doctors at the center were performing unnecessary heart operations to cash in on Medicare payments and to show corporate growth. Kurt Eichenwald of the *New York Times* describes what led to the scandal:

> Until federal agents raided Redding last fall, Tenet's business model was based on maximizing the dollars it could collect from Medicare, the nation's biggest buyer of health care. And Medicare's complex formulas—the template for private insurers, as well—reward some kinds of health care more richly than others, and few more richly than cardiac care....
>
> So it was that two heart doctors at Redding...became immensely

powerful, people who worked there said. Tenet promised investors growing profits, and at Redding, these people said, that required steady growth in cardiac care.[44]

When patients began discovering that they had been, or were about to be, cut open without due cause, whistles sounded and investigations began. In August 2003, Tenet agreed to pay $54 million "to resolve accusations that Redding Medical doctors conducted unnecessary heart procedures and operations on hundreds of healthy patients." Greed was, of course, the issue here, but it was the particular form of greed that gratifies itself by imitating the popular Wall Street model of growth.

Different hospitals can be run more efficiently, but ultimately, health care is a commodity; the science available at one hospital is the same across the street. The industry itself is ancient. Old markets are not supposed to grow as fast as new ones. Yet Wall Street expects and rewards the same sort of double-digit earnings growth from hospital companies that it expects from new and developing businesses. "'The hospital industry is by its very nature a mature industry,' said Mr. [Uwe] Reinhardt, the Princeton economist. 'It is not a high-margin business. It can't be a growth industry like some Internet company. That is just unreasonable.'"[45] Reinhardt's sensible assumption that some businesses, like forest trees, "mature" and no longer can be expected to grow has, up to now, proven a bit too mature for Wall Street and its customers.

Culture. Douthwaite argues that growth is not an economic necessity in nonindustrialized communities. Take, for example, the Indian state of Kerala:

> The Keralans have a long history of educating women, hence its high literacy levels and its declining population—the average is just 1.7 children per family—again a European level. So economic growth is not necessary to get countries through the demographic transition, as has been maintained. Professor William Alexander, who has studied Kerala, thinks much of its success is linked to its matrilineal

social structure. Instead of a top-down structure with long command chains and little feedback from those at the bottom, it has a flat structure that makes for more efficient resource use.

So Kerala's case provides material for the argument that growth is not necessary. If we had a better distribution of income, if the resources being used to generate growth were instead used to provide directly for those at the bottom of the social system, then the results would be much better than relying on "increasing the size of the pie" and "trickle-down" theories.[46]

Here, however, we have a nonindustrialized society, and Douthwaite is quick to admit that industrialized societies need growth of some sort. But this brings up another issue. Is future industrialization a fact of life for *all* cultures? Must the Keralans change their winning ways, and if so, why? Paul Theroux, whose travels in Africa were the basis for his book *Dark Star Safari,* has returned with the impression that many grassroots African cultures want neither to be industrialized nor to be Westernized at all. Here is a section of his NPR interview with Robert Siegel:

> SIEGEL: It's much more fashionable nowadays to say Africans have the same political and material aspirations as anyone else in the world. We just have to get the right relationship between the marketplace and the government and the other institutions, like public health education. You're saying something different. You're saying, for whatever reasons, the aspirations that people bring to life are quite different in much of Africa.
>
> THEROUX: I think that—I mean, we tend to impose our will on Africans and our dreams and our hopes and, I think, subvert their ambitions. But in general, rural Africa, living through the seasons— planting, gleaning, harvesting and whatever—is going on just as it has for hundreds, if not thousands, of years.

Though Westerners have much that non-Westerners might want, it is both incorrect and dangerous to assume that all nations must and will follow a Western path. We do exactly this when we use phrases like *preindustrialized nations* and *developing countries* (a slip made even by the vigorously antigrowth Douthwaite).

Natural Curbs. Growth predictors seldom factor in vectors that operate quite naturally in growth situations. One of these vectors might be called the *value curb*. When a stock's price rises, all else being equal, the stock becomes less and less of a bargain; when the price falls, the stock becomes more and more of a bargain. Thus market trends tend to be self-curbing rather than unregulated. Value curbs can operate with all sorts of growth. In the 1960s, it was *très chic* to sip coffee at Les Deux Magots across from Ste. Germaine in Paris. Then Les Deux Magots started showing up in tourist guides, and the price of a café au lait went through the roof. Suddenly, Les Deux Magots was no longer a fashionable dive. The waters of its exoticism had been fished out.

A second natural curb might be called *growth disease*. Corporations that grow massively and quickly will seldom have time to develop self-regulatory infrastructures and intracommunicative systems, the lack of which exposes these companies to a multitude of risks. Consider the misfortunes of three high-tech golden girls: Oracle, Sun Microsystems, and Microsoft. One company overstated its profits, the next overdiversified, and the third failed to develop an antitrust mechanism. All three of these problems were caused by growth without structure, and all three served to limit growth. Such natural curbs operated even more dramatically on Enron and Global Crossing and many other corporations that did not survive the disease of growth.

Natural curbs can teach us something about growth. Though growth per se is a morally neutral phenomenon, it is full of danger to itself and to the world at large. To work for society, growth must not only integrate with its social and natural environment but also develop its own unique internal awareness. Growth must limit and refine itself in order to endure.

Climax Economics. We return to the virgin forest and walk deeper into it. Towering 225 feet above us, tossing their heads in the mountain winds, are Douglas firs, which share the forest with small shrubs, a 20- to 30-foot-tall undergrowth of smaller trees, and a diverse population of fauna. This is known to biologists as a *climax forest:* an ecosystem in which the dominant species exist in harmony with each other. Especially dramatic in this harmony is the role of the massive firs. Unlike almost everything else alive (cancer, of course, excepted), the Douglas fir has no genetic limiter of growth or life. The tree keeps growing and growing and growing, sometimes for centuries and to heights of over 300 feet, until forces of nature like disease, lightning, or its own colossal mass take it down. The climax forest has found a natural way to endure and even profit from these heroics.

Can a complex economic system function in this way? In other words, can certain economic entities maintain the function of growth, while others contribute to balance and stability? This counterpoint, coupled with the inevitable mortality of some entities, might ensure for us a better alternative to the self-defeating strategy of unlimited growth. It might also prove an appropriate context for the implementation of Serageldin's theory of the four capitals.

Technology and Vulgarity

How does it feel to be vulgar? Asking the question, we miss the point. That vulgarian yakking into his cell phone next to you on the beach is not thinking, "Ah, how deliciously vulgar I'm being." He's simply thinking about what he's doing. The hallmarks of vulgarity are self-obsession and unawareness of context.

Thus the cell phone, for all its intrusive potential, is not a vulgar instrument until it is put to vulgar use. On the other hand, we can call the cell phone a *vulgarizing idea,* because it carries with it the temptation, even the provocation, to behave objectionably in public.

We may lump the cell phone with the all-terrain vehicle (ATV), the Jet Ski, the car stereo, the PDA (personal digital assistant), the handheld game, the earphones, and the laptop as a nuisance group of machines: devices that invite their users to disturb nature, disrupt public space, or do both.

Yet even these machines can interact with their environment in surprising ways. The surf rescue station at Kamaole Beach on the island of Maui is equipped with a pair of Jet Skis and an ATV. These allow the lifeguards to answer distress signals, which can be over ten miles away. It is impressive to see this cheerful bunch in action. The ATV tows a trailer-borne Jet Ski from the garage to the ocean in under a minute. The trailer is disconnected from the ATV and rolled into the water. A lifeguard jumps onto the Jet Ski, revs it, and pops it off the trailer. To see her, clad in the Maui colors of red and yellow, heading off across the ocean on a mission of mercy with spray flying behind her, is to remember knightly missions long past.

Something similar inheres in the pickup truck culture of Maui. American TV ads mainly market full size V-8 pickups, whose styling is a blatant appeal to vulgar yearnings for power and control. The Mauian pickup, on the other hand, is almost always a comparatively humble compact version, usually powered by a modest four-cylinder engine. The body language of these little trucks can be summed up in one word—*work*—because people who did not need these vehicles for work would have no reason to use them at all. Work for a Mauian often means direct contact with the land, because the island flora is so overwhelming as to demand attention from professional and homeowner alike. This shared concern with work and nature has produced a kind of chivalry, a tacit public understanding, among pickup truck drivers. They tend to treat each other with special courtesy and will often greet each other when passing on country roads. Thus, contact with machines can humanize as well as vulgarize.

Compare this with how technology affects middle-class American children. If they live in a typical subdivision, they inhabit a house whose construction has destroyed nature and whose architecture does its best to minimize contact with nature. They are driven to school and home in the family SUV, maybe one of those new ones that look like nasty war machines. You won't find any river mud or rhinoceros dents on this SUV, because it has never been farther than the country club, but you *will* find an inboard DVD and a dashboard navigation system (one subdivision looks so much like another!). The kids' life is so electronic that you would think they had been born with built-in pop-outs and USB connections. The children ease their tensions after strenuous work at school by playing electronic games, enjoying earphone music, and surfing the TV channels. For serious business, however, they turn to the Internet and get to work swapping tunes, games, and porn.

After several years of this regime, parents may discover that their kids look kind of vague, can't participate in social activities, and have lots of trouble concentrating on anything. Doctors inform the worried couple that the problem is attention deficit/hyperactivity disorder (ADHD), an act of God, of course, and prescribe the appropriate drugs.

Doctors and social workers call such events, and the even worse things that are happening to our children, "unfortunate" and "tragic." Why don't we, for a change, call them criminally vulgar? Why don't we brand the parents with old-fashioned shame and reprobation and send the marketers scurrying to their lawyers? I guess we're just not the type for placing blame.

We may conclude that, though many machines are still used to good effect, proliferating technology threatens to vulgarize our society by disrupting our children's growth, alienating us from nature, and denying us the opportunity to practice humanity. While many new machines are marketed as conveniences or pleasures, they function instead as controllers and blinders, keeping us from direct contact with society and nature, robbing us of essential life challenges and distracting us from consciousness of the world. In so doing, they present the most profound of spiritual intrusions possible, the infiltration of market vectors into our core of being.[47]

The Body Vulgar

It is familiar to hear vulgarity linked to the human body, as though enjoyment of the body were something low and vile. The opposite is more likely to be true. Vulgarity obviously touches on the body and its pleasures, but vulgarity in fact separates us from our bodies by turning them into commodities and products. Take the fitness-machine industry, whose two look-alike, sound-alike leaders, Crossbow and Bowflex, run continuous ads on late-night TV. Crossbow presents its product exclusively in terms of the sexy appearance you will achieve after using it:

> MEN: Strength training builds bigger, thicker muscles through low repetitions and high resistance. Plus, you'll achieve that lean, sculpted look you've always dreamed of thanks to the superior fat burning results attributed to a proper strength training workout.

> WOMEN: Strength training with high repetitions and low resistance produces long, lean, beautiful muscles in women. You'll burn fat and uncover muscle tone without getting bulky.

A Bowflex endorsement is more specific:

> Hi, I have been using the Bowflex for 6 months now I started at 130 pounds max and have worked up to 260 pounds max. It is unbelievable. I never ever thought that my strenght [sic] could double 2x in 6 months but with my Bowflex I look good now and I like it. Hehe I am proud to take off my shirt now at the beach and be checkin out some hotties hehe . . . [48]

Let's ignore the question of whether you can look "thicker" and "lean" at the same time, or whether somebody who describes women as "hotties" should have beach privileges at all. We have more serious business here. Deciphering the target language, we conclude that Crossbow and Bowflex are pitching to young to middle-aged consumers, whom the companies encourage to conceive of fitness as a ticket to eroticism. A no-no? Not at all. But just remember that in connecting these two ideas, and these two only, the advertisers are keeping mum about the many *non-erotic* benefits of fitness, as well as the many *non-fitness-related* aspects of eros. The marketers are also touting the body as a commodity in the market of mutual consent.

This brings us right downtown, to that center of commercial activity, the corner of Sex and Market. Beneath the hubbub of booths and stalls, the array of pills, perfumes, instruments, lubricants, protectants, pharmaceuticals, soaps, shampoos, cosmetics, jewelry, body metal, self-help books, videos, CDs, DVDs, linen, and mountains of clothing, run two subtexts. One is for women:

> *Erotic attractiveness is the be-all and end-all. Possessing it is the ticket to good times. Having it will bring you wonderful men. Even if having sex somehow fails to fulfill you, being attractive will keep your husband's attention. And even when you're not with your husband, being attractive will increase your self-esteem and bring you power in the world around you. But Mother Nature just can't do it all, gal. Men like all the bells and whistles.*

The other is for men:

> *Having sex with an attractive woman is the be-all and end-all. The rest of life is mere fluff. But gals are sort of like cars, don't you think? Would you rather have a Plain Jane, or wouldn't you rather get one that's fully loaded?*

We need not be overly outraged by these messages, or even their business purport: *"Buy, buy, you ninnies!"* After all, isn't sex itself a kind of market, an evolutionary bazaar that finances the world with babies? The only problem is that the marketing of the body can backfire. If you ever tried kissing somebody and almost drowned in goo, you get the idea. Sex itself, with all its mysterious complexity and all its transfiguring simplicity, can get drowned in goo. Love can be marketed to death. This begins to happen when women and men present themselves not as individuals but as market artifacts, and when TV reality series pig out on voyeurism.

Vested Interests and Environmental Vulgarity

It happens now and then that institutions and industries, created to serve society, end up serving themselves. Christianity started with the dramatic ministry of a single individual, but by 1300, it was an international corporation, and the pope was declaring political hegemony over all of Europe.[49] Microsoft was born in a garage, but within a generation was richer than many whole nations and asserted imperial power in the marketplace. Phenomena of this sort are connected with growth. As institutions grow, they become wealthier and more powerful. As they swell in size, they develop internal authority structures to confer and apply their power. The individuals in these power structures form networks of vested interests, whose selfish goal is to retain, confirm, and increase the power of the institution at large. The church or corporation no longer sees itself as a tributary to society. The organization has become an entity in itself and for itself.

This cycle is the preamble to corruption. Dominant corporations become money castles that must be defended by any means possible. The corporate entity is an end unto itself; the end justifies any means. Authorities are bribed. Rebels and interlopers are crushed. Plain facts give way to a medley of euphemisms, omissions, and equivocations. Account books read like fairy tales.

Effects of this sort have characterized the activities of the American oil industry over the past few decades. Oilmen are no pikers; they think in trillions. If there has ever been anything like a mother church of the American economy, it is Big Oil. And Big Oil has behaved accordingly. With its galaxy of affiliates—carmakers, airlines, railroads, the military, energy companies, and numerous subsidiaries—Big Oil has used its massive influence vigorously to resist the development of alternative energy sources and the implementation of environmental reforms, even when the fate of the nation lies in the balance. How does Big Oil publicly justify its hegemony? Its trump debating card, played with soporific regularity, is

"Gas is cheap." This morsel of apparent street wisdom has regularly interrupted debate and slowed research.

I say "apparent" because the statement is at best a half-truth. The gas station price of refined oil is nothing like its real cost to the consumer. In 1998, when the price of unleaded was about a dollar, a liberal watchdog group called the International Center for Technology Assessment (CTA) issued a figure-loaded report entitled "The Real Price of Gas." The center estimated that, factoring in "(1) Tax Subsidization of the Oil Industry; (2) Government Program Subsidies; (3) Protection Costs Involved in Oil Shipment and Motor Vehicle Services; (4) Environmental, Health, and Social Costs of Gasoline Usage; and (5) Other Important Externalities of Motor Vehicle Use" (many of which estimates varied broadly), the real cost to the consumer was $5.60 to $15.14 per gallon.

The CTA report, while insightful, fails to be fully convincing, because it is guilty of some liberal rhapsodics. On top of the evidence of the aforementioned hidden expenses, the report provides some much softer figures derived from such fossil-fuel consequences as air pollution, traffic jams, environmental degradation, and urban sprawl. These ballpark figures are much less effective arguments than the tax breaks, subsidies, and protection expenses that the CTA report so ably documents. The disparity between hard and soft figures makes the report look inconsistent and robs it of public-forum bite. (For the executive summary of the report, see the appendix.)

The irony is that, even if the CTA had omitted its softer estimates, it would have come up with some shocking figures. By my estimate, the inclusion of tax breaks, program subsidies, and protection would give us hidden costs of $0.60 to $1.00 per gallon, a 60–100 percent tax kicker. If the CTA had announced that Americans were actually paying $1.60 to $2.00, instead of a mere $1.00, per gallon in 1998, and then discussed the other hidden costs without using dollar figures, the organization might have made waves and brought about some public action.

What has all this to do with vulgarity? The big-business lie about the real price of gas was vulgar in two important ways: It vulgarized consumers by withholding critical knowledge, and it promoted environmental vulgarity by ensuring years of continued air pollution. The world of 2006 (in which, by the way, the 1998 price of unleaded has now more than doubled) owes its poor record in gas economy and environmental protection in part to the glib corporate fiction that "gas is cheap."

The Balance of Nature

We began this chapter in a forest that symbolized the balance of nature, and we have since passed through four episodes of the subversion of balance by self-absorbed human markets. These destabilizing influences will continue to work until their dangers are brought to national awareness by responsible individuals. Walk in a virgin forest someday, and remember that the woods would not be there at all if conscientious people, provoked by love of the land, had not worked for years and taken considerable heat to preserve this land. It is people like this, if anyone at all, who will reconcile us with nature and balance our society.

CHAPTER SIX

A FOOTNOTE ON VULGARITY AND CRIME

Vulgarity is so variously and intimately intertwined with crime that it is almost impossible to consider the two phenomena separately. Most crimes are, in fact, acts of vulgarity—compulsive grabs for the quick fix, deeds sprung from the obsession for control, initiatives conceived in a vacuum of human continuity. We will see later (Chapter 7) that Homer, the earliest maven of Western culture, makes little or no distinction between vulgarity and evil. We have already seen, moreover, that large-scale crimes derived from vulgar instincts can succeed only if the perpetrators vulgarize their victims. The tobacco industry killed millions by fostering addiction and withholding critical information. Fast-food purveyors have killed millions by manipulating habit-forming chemicals and keeping customers in the dark about it. A vulgarized version of the "growth model" provoked an epidemic of white-collar crime and caused surgeons to perform a series of totally unnecessary operations. Vulgarity causes crime by limiting our options, sapping our integrity, blinding us to context, and starving us of consciousness.

Yet American society, even at its most liberal, can be unaware of just how this harm is done. Take Michael Moore's sprawling cinematic tirade *Bowling for Columbine* (2002). Moore uses the April 20, 1999, Columbine High School shootings in Jefferson County, Colorado, as the springboard for a lengthy inquiry into the issue of America's comparatively high rate of violent crime. At first he seems satisfied with the simplistic answer that crime is caused by our abundant availability of firearms; he offers us scene after scene of guns popping off, sometimes harmlessly and sometimes fatally, in what must be all of the fifty states. But then he hits a contradiction. Canada, too, has a liberal supply of guns (7 million weapons for its 10 million families), but no serious problem with violent crime. Why, then, are Americans so much more violent than Canadians? Moore resorts to the convenient, if tenuous, argument that Americans live in "a culture of fear," which, apparently, makes them so edgy, suspicious, and vituperative that they polish each other off in droves.

Fear? I almost wish that America's high rate of violent crime could be ascribed to that single cause. But major indicators suggest that, even after 9/11, America remains the most complacent and self-absorbed nation on earth. Millions of us pay good money at the theater just to be frightened by Hannibal or Freddie. Moore has oversimplified and misfired. But "culture of fear" is a catchy phrase. It might work on North Korea.

Michael Moore ought simply to have looked around him. To explore something as subtle as the causes of social violence, one must examine infrastructures, detail by detail. One must learn to consider these infrastructures as conduits for human liberty or imprisonment. Moore might have noticed the dehumanizing scale of Columbine High School, its corridors wide enough to accommodate two thousand students milling from class to class. He might have studied the school curriculum, which came under fire for lack of moral substance soon after the shootings. He might have looked out from the schoolyard to see the Denver suburbs like Littleton (population 40,000) burgeoning over the valley and up to the Front Range, strangling the valley with their highways, shading the mountain air with car exhaust. He might have considered that other highway, the Internet, where the two young killers, Eric Harris and Dylan Klebold, supposedly under the supervision of their parents, consumed the messages of hate that impelled them to action. Moore might have discussed the in-school cliques whose members verbally abused Harris and Klebold. He might have noted that the Columbine culture was so culturally provincial that fellow students actually autographed the coffins of the slain. He might have found it interesting that Columbine High School deans, months before the shootings, chose to suppress the news that Eric Harris was making bombs.[50]

These readings suggest simple-enough answers. When we put children in schools that are large and crowded, we make children feel small and insignificant. When we pave over the children's valley, we make them feel walled in. When we substitute the mall for the village, we rob children's lives of character and diversity. When we fail to require a core of humanities studies, we rob children of the basis for taste and standards. When we deprive children's lives of character, they may manufacture their own character by forming extreme and exclusionist cliques. And when we not only create and tolerate these conditions, but also fail to supervise or challenge children, then we are sure to see bad things fill the spiritual vacuum that we have created. When we vulgarize our infrastructures, we can expect major grief.

Granted, this grief will not always show up as homicidal crime. But less sensational forms of crime, because they are far more epidemic, are comparably harmful. Take a Columbine graduate, already the victim of mass management, impoverishment of character, and lack of leadership, set him or her down in an "adult" marketplace that is dominated by corporate bottom-lining, and the results are not likely to be inspirational. A feckless education and a greedy marketplace are the only necessary ingredients for white-collar crime.

Which brings us back to Michael Moore and *Bowling for Columbine*. Moore's film has been praised as an act of liberalism, when instead we may ask whether *Bowling* is not a form of liberal vulgarity: the tendency to brainstorm rather than observe, the choice of a sexy quick-fix explanation (the "culture of fear") over the challenging process of social analysis. Liberal bluster of this sort leaves the real task of liberalism—reform through understanding—to the community at large, and sometimes the results can be surprising. Take that promising initiative in American education, New

Visions for Public Schools, as described in a September 2003 *New York Times* editorial:

> New York City is in the forefront of a national movement aimed at converting large, factory-style schools that often have thousands of students into smaller public schools where students have closer contact with teachers. The small-schools movement got a big boost yesterday, when the Bill & Melinda Gates Foundation announced that it would provide seven nonprofit organizations across the city with $51.2 million, with the aim of creating 67 new schools along those lines. . . . National data on small schools shows that they tend to be quieter and safer, with fewer dropouts and higher graduation rates.

New Visions for Public Schools is supported not only by the Gates Foundation and the Carnegie Corporation, but also, among others, by the New York Life Insurance Company, J. P. Morgan Chase, and Citicorp.

New Visions for Public Schools is a quietly run organization. Though in place since 1989, it has received only twenty-one thousand hits on the Internet, compared with 2.4 million for *Bowling for Columbine*. But the initiative's activities suggest that at places like MetLife, Citicorp, and Microsoft, there are people who know a bit more than Michael Moore about social infrastructures and their effects on young minds.

To compare New Visions for Public Schools with *Bowling for Columbine* is to understand why the growth of American self-awareness is so agonizingly slow. The obvious preconditions of crime—convenient handguns, addiction, poverty, and the other usual suspects—have been and will remain targets of opportunity for short-term journalistic treatments and works of social sensationalism. Limiting crime through enforcement and regulation may well pacify society, but it will not touch the root cause of the problem: the gaping want of substance in the upbringing of our young. We will not effectively speak to this issue until we have elevated American education from a baseline necessity to a task-force priority.

Part Two

THE
CHALLENGE
OF
CONSCIOUSNESS

CONSCIOUSNESS AS LIBERATION

One of the most typically vulgar acts I've ever seen was committed by a prince. His instrument, or rather weapon, was a brand new Mercedes 300 SL convertible. He left this car just in front of his college dormitory, motor running, driver's door ajar, stereo blaring rock and roll at full volume, and the car remained so for the better part of an hour.

Trivial? Of course, but some of the most provocative pictures are painted in miniature. The prince's behavior displayed in the purest form both his disregard for others and his compulsive need to display it, a form of vulgarity as self-damaging as it was offensive. This arrogance was also characteristic of his family's regime. It collapsed within twenty years, leaving the family members dead or in exile.

The prince was an ignorant, spoiled brat who took liberties. Vulgarity is liberty without consciousness. Just as conscious liberty creates the best of worlds, unconscious liberty creates the worst.

But what is consciousness? Imagine that you are a twelve-year-old girl in Channelview, Texas (see Chapter 3), and that your "culture"—the values and language inhering in your small branch of society—is dominated by athletics and cheerleading. The cultural sun rises and sets on cheerleading. Girls practice cheerleading moves at home, on the way to school, and in the halls. To be selected for the cheerleading team is every girl's dream, and not to be selected is the most miserable form of failure conceivable. You are a member of this culture, and consequently, you are locked up in its compulsive enthusiasm and appalling tunnel vision.

But one morning, you wake up and sense that something has

changed profoundly. The morning sunlight is projecting the moving shadows of leaves upon your bedroom wall, and the free play of light and shadow fascinates you in a completely new way. What has caused the change? Was it something a teacher said yesterday or something you read last night? Whatever it was, you suddenly realize that there is a world out there beyond cheerleading and that in fact this other world may be full of things far more important, urgent, and wonderful.

You feel exhilarated and a bit scared. Your insight has simultaneously liberated you from a closed paradigm and alienated you from your classmates.

Consciousness, as I define it, is precisely this form of liberation. It comprises the ability to see the details of life from a broader perspective. This expanded perspective includes your lifetime goals, your concept of serious achievement, your place in history, your view of your own social order, your self-inquiry. The specific details of life—short-term goals, local paradigms, data, theories, methods—take on positive or negative meaning only when reviewed from this inclusive continuum.

This sort of consciousness can be hard to achieve, but once achieved, it is infectious. It adds a new vitality to life and injects underlying energy that invests day-to-day activity with a new drama. You yearn to share this energy with others by finding like-minded friends, by teaching, and by child-rearing. You desire to focus your new awareness on professional and social issues.

Because of its liberating powers, consciousness is the opposite of vulgarity and the antidote for it. Only by looking beyond the immediate can we distinguish waste from investment, harmful habits from healthy pursuits. We may still make mistakes or be forced to choose the lesser of two evils. But even these misfortunes can be of some value. Consciousness learns and remembers.

CHAPTER SEVEN

HOMER AND THE BIRTH OF CONSCIOUSNESS

Vulgarity and Evil: From Bush to Homer

On January 29, 2002, President George W. Bush famously referred to Iraq, North Korea, and Iran as an "axis of evil" threatening world order. In so doing, he invoked a Christian idea of evil—an idea that is dauntingly complex, including, as it does, everything from sexual indulgence to diabolical genius. Not all Americans, or even all Christians, are at ease with this idea. It has been criticized as being outmoded or subjective or both. How it relates to American vulgarity will concern us in this chapter.

On earlier pages, I have connected vulgarity with evil. But to say that everything vulgar is evil is incorrect. To pig out on a triple burger with supersized fries is vulgar, very vulgar, but not evil. On the other hand, to say that everything evil is vulgar is, at least, a useful hypothesis. The murderous zealots who destroy civilian life in the name of God or nation are demonstrably vulgar. The cynical leaders who educate and incite them celebrate and participate in vulgarity. Evildoers may behave like sophisticates, but the crowd speaks in their actions. The elegant Count Dracula, after all, was at root nothing more than a cannibal on fluids. The heart of evil—disregard for humanity and nature—is also the heart of vulgarity.

To see this connection in action, we need only look back to a period of history when the modern Judeo-Christian idea of evil was not yet in place: the world of the poet Homer. Homer's *Iliad* is a tragedy with no real villain, a narrative whose major figures—Agamemnon, Priam, Achilles, and Hector—are all heroic and all doomed. With only two exceptions (to be discussed a bit later), Homer's values are based exclusively on Greek skills and endowments: valor in battle, eloquence in council, beauty, technical mastery. Conversely, his most stinging moral reproach is for Thersites, a Greek who is conspicuously lacking in excellence of any kind:

> Now all the rest sat down and kept their place upon the benches, only Thersites still chattered on, the uncontrolled speech, whose mind was full of words many and disorderly, wherewith to strive against the chiefs idly and in no good order, but even as he deemed that he should make the Argives laugh. And he was ill-favored beyond all men that came to Ilios. Bandy-legged was he, and lame of one foot, and his two shoulders rounded, arched down upon his chest; and over them his head was warped, and a scanty stubble sprouted on it. Hateful was he to Achilles above all and to Odysseus, for them he was wont to revile. But now with shrill shout he poured forth his upbraidings upon goodly Agamemnon.[51]

Four times, Homer hammers away at Thersites' clumsy speech ("chattered on," "uncontrolled speech," "words many and disorderly," "idly and in no good order"). Five times, he takes aim at Thersites' physical appearance (legs, foot, shoulders, head, hair). These shortcomings are crowned by Thersites' disrespect for virtue (Achilles, Odysseus) and his attack on civic order (King Agamemnon). The implications are clear enough: Misfortune and civil disorder are linked to people who lack the skills of humanity, people who cannot put ideas together, people who act on intemperate impulse rather than evolved consideration. Homer is linking evil with ignorance and vulgarity.

This idea becomes thematic in Homer's *Odyssey*. Unlike *The Iliad*, *The Odyssey* is a thoroughly moral work that returns again and again to the dos and don'ts of human speech and action. In meetings with divinity, human beings, and even animals, Odysseus' prudence and fortitude come under scrutiny, and he returns the favor by testing the characters he runs into. Unlike *The Iliad*, *The Odyssey* has a definite set of villains: Penelope's infamous suitors, who infest Odysseus' palace in his absence, flouting the rules of hospitality and literally eating away at his estate. Finally, *The Odyssey* contains a moral allegory, the first of its kind in Western literature. Odysseus' fanciful adventures with Calypso, Aeolus, Scylla, and Charybdis are full of symbolism and allusion relating to human vices and virtues. There are the Sirens, the Lotus Eaters, and the enchantress Circe, whose charms turn men into swine—all parables of the vulgarizing and paralyzing effects of short-term pleasures:

> She showed them to thrones and seats and confected for them a mess of cheese with barley-meal and clear honey, mulched in Pramnian wine. With this she mixed drugs so sadly powerful as to steal from them all memory of their native land. After they had drunk from the cup she struck them with her wand; and straightway hustled them to her sties, for they grew the heads and shapes and bristles of swine, with swine-voices too.[52]

But Odysseus' most terrifying escapade, his imprisonment in the cave of the giant Cyclops, is Homer's best shot at describing absolute evil. Here again—and this time with supernatural trappings—evil is related to vulgarity. Before the adventure, Odysseus has a premonition that he will meet "a strange man, clothed in mighty strength, one *that knew not judgment and justice*" (italics mine). When he later meets and speaks to the single-eyed Cyclops, the monster boasts that he would not, "to shun the enmity of Zeus, spare either thee or thy company, unless my spirit bade me," meaning in context that the Cyclops respects the laws neither of gods nor of men. The Cyclops then grabs two of Odysseus' men, brains them, cuts them up, and eats them:

> His savagery disdained me one word in reply. He leapt to his feet, lunged with his hands among my fellows, snatched up two of them like whelps and rapped their heads against the ground. The brains burst from their skulls and were spattered over the cave's floor, while he broke them up, limb from limb, and supped off them to the last

shred, eating ravenously like a mountain lion, everything—bowels and flesh and bones, even to the marrow of the bones.

(*The Odyssey*, book 9)

As the crafty Odysseus plies the Cyclops with strong wine, the giant asks his name. To protect himself from future retribution, the hero adopts history's first nom de guerre, "Noman." This satisfies the Cyclops, who is getting thoroughly drunk.

He sprawled full-length, belly up, on the ground, lolling his fat neck aside; and sleep that conquers all men conquered him. Heavily he vomited out all his load of drink, and gobbets of human flesh swimming in wine spurted gurgling from his throat.

Odysseus and his men blind the monster with a sharpened and heated log that sizzles in the eye socket. Afterwards, the Greeks escape under the Cyclops' sheep when the animals are sent out to pasture. Once in his ship again, Odysseus hurls an insult back at his attacker:

"So, Cyclops, you were unlucky and did not quite have the strength to eat all the followers of this puny man within your cave? Instead the luck returned your wickedness upon itself in fit punishment for the impiety that had dared eat the guests in your house."

A moral tale if ever there was one! But an especially Greek moral tale. The Cyclops is the absolute vulgarian: deaf to the justice of gods or men, pitiless, ugly, cannibalistic, and deficient in table manners. He is too much of an oaf to understand a simple joke, and worst of all, he is heartless to his guests. He is unconscious of humanity and devoid of culture. He is Homer's version of the Lowest of the Low. Fittingly, the Cyclops is conquered by Homer's avatar of culture and consciousness, Odysseus of the Many Counsels. Homer presents us with an idea of culture and consciousness as virtue.

The moral values of *The Odyssey* were an early and influential example of what would become the moral values of Greece and

Rome. These values, by and large, amounted to an assertion of a just and literate culture. The gods deserved ceremonial respect, but spirituality as we now know it was simply not on the table. The core of morality was civic, and civic virtue was built on moderation, prudence, fortitude, decorum, literacy, and eloquence. Earthly pleasures were to be gratified in measure, and the punishment for lack of measure was not religious guilt but rather civic shame.

The education for this life was a curriculum that became known in ancient Rome as the *Artes Liberales*, the basis for which came down to modern times as the liberal arts. But these arts were only for the ruling minority of the state. After all, why should a shopkeeper or a farmer learn how to defend a legal case or lead men in battle? The idea that a version of the *Artes Liberales* might enlighten the citizens and strengthen the state simply did not occur to the authorities. Without the challenge and enablement of education, the majority of the voting public subsided into a vulgarity that would ultimately ruin the republic, spread into imperial palaces, and undo Rome.

But (Edward Gibbon notwithstanding) Rome never really fell. As its pagan institutions declined, they were replaced by the Christian institutions of a church that would ultimately take on its own trappings of empire. The passing of rule from pagan to Christian values was characterized by three major distinctions:

1. Although the church was subject to the state in ancient Rome, the Christian Church would claim a position at the core of culture and politics.

2. While pagans were taught to live in the here and now, Christians were taught to devalue the things of this world in favor of a life of the spirit.

3. While ancient Roman values were nation-centered and aristocratic, Christian values were universalist and democratic.

This new Rome, this Christian revolution, relates to vulgarity and the idea of evil in fascinating if sometimes unsettling ways. As a religious movement, Christianity did not reach out to critical thinkers and questioning minds. Its promise of community, spirituality, and the immediate fix of conversion appealed directly to the disenfranchised and uneducated masses. Thus, its effect on Roman vulgarity was equivocal. Christianity reformed and refined Rome, and ultimately all of Europe, by revealing a second, nonmaterial dimension in life, a spiritual world holding a boundless plenty of togetherness, forgiveness, and love. But the Christian Church maintained and in fact exploited European vulgarity by suppressing doctrinal diversity, discouraging education, and stifling free thought. Add to this an irrationally severe moral code; a creed based on primitive writings; a set of palpable fictions supported by unctuous sophistry; a papacy often greedy for political power; repeated priestly abuses; and a huge miscellany of angels, saints, icons, and relics, and you have vulgarization on a substantial scale.

The same paradox applies today. Most American churches are islands of civility in a hurried and venal culture. But by the same token, most American churches are deserts in terms of cultural literacy and free inquiry. American churchgoers tend to vote for father figures, flag wavers, and fellow churchgoers. They chose the marginally literate, Bible-packing George W. Bush first over his more thoughtful and freethinking fellow Republican, John McCain, and then (in a disputed vote-count) over the admittedly capable Democrat, Al Gore. They elected and then reelected the man who appealed to their faith and indulged their ignorance.

Religious anti-intellectualism, and efforts by the church to preserve it, have much to do with the development of the Christian idea of evil. Because the church stifled dissent and characterized the pursuit of worldly knowledge as sinful, the traditional Christian idea of evil is tinged with a fear of the alien and the unknown. The Devil, that brilliant Christian hoax, is known as a keeper of secrets, a secret in and of himself, a fearsome, exotic icon worshiped by secret societies. Jews were regarded as evil secret-keepers. Nontraditional healers were persecuted as witches. Science was decried as anathema. Even women were portrayed, by an energetic antifeminist tradition, as casting forth an evil aura of sexually forbidden knowledge. This notion of evil was, and (although Christianity has modernized itself) largely remains, a factor in the vulgarization of churchgoers.

We need only look at Christianity's "sister" faith, Islam, to see this problem etched in stone. Like Christianity, Islam offers safe haven and spiritual expression to hundreds of millions of people. But unlike Christianity, Islam has never felt the shock of reform or experienced a relaxation of its original strictures. It remains historically pristine. As in the past, it asserts itself at the heart of politics. Its ancient system, replete with fierce faith, anti-intellectualism, and xenophobia, rudely engages a world of globalization, real time, and information technology. Its madrassas (religious schools) teach reaction, violent hatred, warped history, and abject worship of authority. In its fundamentalist forms, Islam feeds on the vulgarization of the faithful.

Thus, when the U.S. president calls others "evil," he is seen as evil by these others. And as we observe the prejudices of others, so we must also look to our own.

Homage to Peleus:
Literature and the Birth of Social Consciousness

Just as vulgarity does not show its full face without the fear and hatred of strangeness, social consciousness cannot emerge without the acceptance and integration of the strange. The emergence of this form of consciousness is revealed to us in its historical setting by literature. Appropriately, just as it was Homer who spearheaded the attack on vulgarity, it was Homer who first opened the window of social consciousness.

I commented earlier that, with only two exceptions, the values of Homer's *Iliad* were based exclusively on well-established Greek skills and endowments. But these two exceptions are of epochal significance. The first of these is a brief tableau that will lay the foundation for the Greek study of comparative politics. To prepare

Achilles for battle, the god Hephaistos creates a marvelous shield for him, on the face of which he depicts two cities. The first is a city at peace, well ordered and prosperous. There are weddings, feasting, torches, dancing, songs, and the music of viols and flutes. In the assembly place, two parties are disputing "the blood-price of a man slain," but this most divisive of issues is tried and judged in strict decorum by august and authoritative elders:

> And heralds kept order among the folk, while the elders on polished stones were sitting in the sacred circle, and holding in their hands staves from the loud-voiced heralds. Then before the people they rose up and gave judgment each in turn. And in the midst lay two talents of gold, to be given unto him who should plead among them most righteously.   (*The Iliad*, book 18)

The second city is less fortunate:

> But around the other city were two armies in siege with glittering arms. And two counsels found favour among them, either to sack the town or to share all with the townsfolk even whatsoever substance the fair city held within. But the besieged were not yet yielding, but arming for an ambushment. On the wall there stood to guard it their dear wives and infant children, and with these the old men; but the rest went forth, and their leaders were Ares and Pallas Athene, both wrought in gold, and golden was the vesture they had on.   (ibid.)

This second city is defended by warriors who ambush, spy on, pillage from, and heartlessly slaughter their own people. Speedily they are engaged by the enemy, and the resultant action is the embodiment of chaos:

> And among them mingled Strife and Tumult, and fell Death, grasping one man alive fresh-wounded, another without wound, and dragging another dead through the mellay by the feet; and the raiment on her shoulders was red with the blood of men. Like living mortals they hurled together and fought, and haled the corpses each of the other's slain.   (ibid.)

Note that in his description of the first city, Homer carefully details the infrastructure of rational politics: law, information flow ("the loud-voiced heralds"), executive government, the arts, eloquence, and participatory citizenship. The description begins with a wedding celebration, symbolizing civic security and continuity into the future. The second city, under siege, lacks all these provisions. It is in dire straits, with its women and children at stake and its enemies already arguing over how to divide the spoils. Its soldiers, instead of facing the enemy, fall upon and slay two civilians. It is paying the penalty for its own bad politics.

Note also that gods are involved on both sides of this war, while in the description of the happy city, no god of any kind is mentioned.

Clearly, the second city represents the world of *The Iliad,* a chaotic struggle typified by deception, competitive heroics, gods in strife, and the absence of civic order. The first city, however, opens like a new window into a saner world. It displays a civility based on wisely ordained institutions and a commitment to reason (no gods necessary here). Homer is looking into a mental landscape that is wholly lacking in the Troy story or in the primitive tribalism that the story depicts. He is looking into the morally charged world of *The Odyssey* and towards the dawn of modern politics. His description of Achilles' shield is an assertion of social consciousness.

The Iliad's second exception conveys an insight so revolutionary that, twenty-seven hundred years later, it still has not been absorbed by some cultures. Late in the poem, Priam, King of Troy, appears in the tent of his Greek arch-enemy, Achilles. Priam pleads with Achilles to release the dead body of Priam's son Hector, whom Achilles has slain. But Achilles refuses stonily. After all, hadn't it been Hector who killed Achilles' own dear friend Patroklos? Priam finally resorts to eloquence, beseeching Achilles to think of his own father, Peleus, who is missing him back in Greece:

> Yea, fear thou the gods, Achilles, and have compassion on me, even me, bethinking thee of thy father. Lo, I am yet more piteous than he,

and have braved what none other man on earth hath braved before,
to stretch forth my hand toward the face of the slayer of my sons.
(ibid., book 24)

Achilles cannot but be moved by this line of argument. He knows,
via prophecy, that he will die at Troy without seeing his own father
again. He realizes that Peleus will soon be lamenting a slain son,
just as Priam is now.

> Thus spake he [Priam], and stirred within Achilles desire to make
> lament for his father. And he touched the old man's hand and gently
> moved him back. And as they both bethought them of their dead,
> so Priam for man-slaying Hector wept sore as he was fallen before
> Achilles' feet, and Achilles wept for his own father, and now again for
> Patroklos, and their moan went up throughout the house.   (ibid.)

Homer here becomes the earliest "citizen of the world." The idea
of two sworn enemies, driven against each other by blood revenge,
weeping and lamenting together, would have been unthinkable
in the vigorous tribalism depicted by *The Iliad*. By actually voicing
this thought, Homer looks beyond that narrow purview, out into
a domain at once more compassionate and more philosophical,
where mankind is all of a piece, consciousness reigns over ignorance, and forms of moral justice are universal.

These new values are made more specific in *The Odyssey*, which
opens with a modernistic manifesto of human autonomy and
responsibility from the lips of Zeus himself:

> "It vexes me to see how mean are these creatures of a day towards
> us gods, when they charge against us the evils (far beyond our worst
> dooming) which their own exceeding wantonness has heaped upon
> themselves."   (*The Odyssey,* book 1)

The entire epic can be read as a postscript to this remark. "Blindness of heart"—passion, greed, and, above all, lack of awareness—
will be abundantly characterized by the Cyclops, Odysseus' men

who are turned into swine by Circe, and the suitors with their non-stop feasting in Odysseus' hall. Odysseus himself, on the other hand, will personify moral vision; he will be the hero of consciousness, the man on whom nothing is lost. He will become the active response to Zeus's assertion of human responsibility.

What is the shape of Odysseus's consciousness? First, he is abundantly literate: the best orator among the Greeks, informed historian, wise counselor, masterful leader, capable sailor, feared warrior, champion athlete. He knows the language of the court, the language of town, the language of the fields. Second, he is emotionally intelligent; he is boundlessly curious, and his feelings run deep, but he has the temperance to control these inner passions and keep them in perspective. Third, he has a sense of purpose, which allows him to distinguish between important goals and temporary distractions and to develop plans patiently in time. Finally, he has savvy: the grace to carry his own talents lightly, the street wisdom to probe the capacity and motivations of the people he must depend on, and the imagination to create, for self-protection, a bodyguard of lies.

Odysseus is thus the heroic embodiment of The Odyssey's new vision. Just as Achilles the Doomed is the model figure for the god-haunted tribal chaos of old Greece, Odysseus the Devious is Homer's candidate for an exclusively human playing-field: newly developing town life and business.

Odysseus reaches his native Ithaca and enters the town disguised as a beggar. As he narrates the hero's meetings with Eumaeus, Telemachus, and the old dog Argos, Homer uses symbol and theme to round out his image of consciousness with two key elements: hospitality in its broadest sense and appreciation for the individual.

Eumaeus' rustic house is the first place Odysseus visits after reaching the shore of Ithaca. The two men knew each other well in the past, but Odysseus' appearance has been altered by Athena, and he does not reveal his identity until he has thoroughly tested Eumaeus' mettle. Odysseus' politely clever cross-examination focuses on two questions: Has Eumaeus been loyal to him in his absence, and how does Eumaeus receive poor strangers? Eumaeus' responses prove that his loyalty and hospitality are unimpeachable. Odysseus' joyous response underlines Homer's concern with the idea of hospitality:

> With no more ado the honest swineherd led him to the inner room and there shook down for him a couch of springy twigs, which he covered with the great thick hairy goat-skin that was his own sleeping-mat. Odysseus rejoiced at being thus received and thanked him saying: "Host, may Zeus and the other immortal gods concede your dearest wish in return for this ready welcome you proffer."
>
> (ibid., book 14)

In Homer's dramatic emphasis on hospitality through this scene, we see a broad-based awareness of shared humanity: generosity, compassion, and acceptance of strangeness. These virtues suggest a modernized society energized by commerce with foreign cities. Additionally, these virtues point to a modernized politics, a liberal culture, and the idea of human equality.

As though in counterpoint to this universalizing theme, Homer then develops the idea of the individual. He does this through a series of poignant scenes in which the long-lost hero is recognized by those who love him. As Odysseus approaches his house in town for the first time since his return, he and Eumaeus pass an old dog:

> As they talked a dog lying there lifted his head and pricked his ears. This was Argos, whom Odysseus had bred but never worked.... So lay Argos on the ground, all shivering with dog-ticks. Yet the instant Odysseus approached, the beast knew him. He thumped his tail and drooped his ears forward, but lacked power to drag himself ever so little towards his master.   (ibid., book 17)

Odysseus in turn recognizes Argos but cannot compromise his own anonymity. Brushing back a tear, he walks on. Exhausted with emotion, Argos dies. Later, Odysseus, still in disguise but now inside his own house, is washed by the elderly maid, Eurycleia, who recognizes him by a scar on his thigh:

> Now as the old woman took up his leg and stroked her hands gently along it she knew the scar by its feel. She let go the foot, which with his shin splashed down into the tub and upset it with a noisy clatter. The water poured over the ground. In Eurycleia's heart such joy and sorrow fought for mastery that her eyes filled with tears and her voice was stifled in her throat. So she caught Odysseus by the beard to whisper, "You are my own child, Odysseus himself, and I never knew—not till I had fondled the body of my King." (ibid., book 19)

And later still, his wife, Penelope, testing Odysseus' real identity, commands Eurycleia to move the royal bed into another room. Odysseus exclaims that the bed cannot be moved, because he himself built it around an olive tree:

> Within our court had sprung a stem of olive, bushy, long in the leaf, vigorous; the bole of it column-thick. Round it I plotted my bed-chamber, walled entire with fine-jointer ashlar and soundly roofed. ... With this [tree] for main member (boring it with my augur wherever required) I went on to frame up the bed, complete; inlaying it with gold, silver and ivory and lacing it across with oxhide thongs, dyed blood-purple. (ibid., book 23)

Convinced at last, Penelope, half-fainting, embraces her husband.

These three recognition scenes, each with its own haunting details, complete Homer's depiction of Odysseus as a unique individual, a nonpareil in terms of his specific talents and passions and quirks. The sense of his uniqueness is intensified rather than weakened when, again and again in the course of his travels, he must assume fake identities, submerging his heroic history and hiding his skills, his honors, and even his good looks. These disguises play out in conjunction with another major signifier of identity: Odysseus' repeated expression of his indomitable passion to return to his land and his people. This tension becomes exquisitely painful when, even after returning to his home, he must temporarily hide his identity from those dearest to him. This self-suppression is prefigured in his self-introduction to the Cyclops as "Noman." But with the final recognitions by Argos, Eurycleia, and Penelope (and the battle scenes that follow), the built-up pressure is released, and Odysseus' identity is realized in its socially completed form. He has revealed and fulfilled himself. He is again Odysseus of Ithaca.

Why is Homer so interested in the individual? Perhaps because the individual, fully developed, self-expressed, and self-realized, can develop only in the Peaceful City, the society that might be built on the new consciousness expressed in *The Odyssey*. Only the Peaceful City can produce citizens who, instead of incessantly responding to war and disorder, can develop individuality by exercising a full set of options. Summarizing the major components of Homeric social consciousness—its sense of transnationality; its awareness of comparative politics; its realization of human autonomy and responsibility; its emphases on self-awareness, literacy, judgment, curiosity, inventiveness, emotional intelligence, savvy, compassion, generosity, and individual identity—we find that Homer has offered us a fairly complete template for individual and social consciousness, and that his work is shockingly modern. And when we reverse the vectors and revisit Homer's images of evil—the Cyclops, Circe, and the insatiable suitors—we find that Homer's definition of the Bad is not some romanticized dark force, but rather, simply put, vulgarity: the proud ignorance, the vulnerability to addiction, the blockish inability and headstrong unwillingness to awaken, to listen, to appreciate, to evolve.

What does all this say about the Judeo-Christian idea of evil, that bugbear of President Bush, that image of a diabolical, mysterious brooding force? It implies that this idea is unnecessarily complicated and may even have been part of a strategy to keep worshipers confused and dependent on the church. Not even all Christian authorities believed in it, anyway. It was Augustine himself who wrote that evil was, purely and simply, the absence of good.[53]

A Consciousness Pill?

Homer's account of vulgarity is as true in America now as it was in Homer's Greece. But now the care and feeding of vulgarity is a trillion-dollar business. Penelope's suitors are into fast foods, the Cyclops ranges the mall, and Circe, in a thousand magical forms, is busily turning us into swine. Homer is not around to sing of a changed society and a new awareness. What is to be done? Should the National Endowment for the Humanities fund ten thousand Homer impersonators to visit classrooms, extolling Odyssean virtue? An interactive *Odyssey* adventure for the Internet? A Hollywood remake of *The Odyssey* with Russell Crowe as the sea-swept hero and *Harry Potter*–style special effects? These are the usual Band-Aids, flimflams that compound the problem by vulgarizing the solution.

Instead we must reassess our culture at its infrastructure. And to do so, we will have to consider a topic that is, in its own way, even more terrible than the Cyclops: American education.

CHAPTER EIGHT

THE EDUCATION
OF THE VULGAR

Not everyone is called to be a physician, a lawyer, a philosopher, to live in the public eye, nor has everyone outstanding gifts of natural capacity, but all of us are created for the life of social duty, all are responsible for the personal influence that goes forth from us.

Vittorino da Feltre (1373–1446)

Is America the empire of vulgarity? Many journalists would seem to think so. Within a single week in January 2005, both the American vice president and the president himself were hauled into the journalistic world court for alleged acts of grossness. Dick Cheney attended the sober Auschwitz Memorial ceremonies in "the kind of attire one typically wears to operate a snow blower," while George Bush's demeanor at his inauguration a few days earlier inspired a tirade entitled "The Emperor of Vulgarity," which characterized him as a

> strutting Texan mountebank, with his chimpanzee smirk and his born-again banalities delivered in that constipated syntax that sounds the way cold cheeseburgers look, and his grinning plastic wife, and his scheming junta of neo-con spivs, shamans, flatterers and armchair warmongers, and his sinuous evasions and his brazen lies, and his sleight of hand theft from the American poor, and his rape of the environment, and his lethal conviction that the world must submit to his Pax Americana or be bombed into charcoal.[54]

Granted, not all journalists take such a dim view of Bush & Co. But just about all have at one point or another held his presidential table manners under scrutiny. The cowboy boots, ideal equipment for the Executive Swagger. The bungled language. The moments of apparent disorientation. And more seriously, the self-righteousness. The religious idolatry. The veneration of Big Money. The dirty tricks. No, George W. Bush may not be wrong about everything, and those who write him off as a mere fool are making a big mistake. But his attitudes and behavior firmly qualify him to be First Citizen of American Vulgar.

Why should the world's leading nation have elected and reelected a man of such debilitating limitations? First off, we must acknowledge the fact of life that presidents who engaged in global conflict have always been reelected unless, like Lyndon Johnson, they chose to step down. But to stop with this explanation is to ignore a huge cultural phenomenon, already alluded to in the preceding chapter: Millions of Americans support George Bush because they think like George Bush. They are bored by information and ignore learning. They seek macho leadership and easy answers to issues. They believe that they have been saved by the Lamb of God.

How did this state of affairs arise? Many causes might be adduced, but at the forefront I would like to suggest two factors that are especially compelling because they seem to be related to each other: the rise of the religious right and the destruction, by the academic left, of American education in the humanities. These two factors and their culturally erosive interaction with each other are illustrated spectacularly by a legal issue that arose in Alabama and soon gained national recognition.

The Case of Justice Moore. The year 2003 saw a momentous but rather embarrassing test of the U.S. Constitutional separation of church and state. Alabama Chief Justice Roy Moore ordered that a two-ton religious monument be placed in the lobby of the Alabama Judicial Building. He used the Declaration of Independence as his authority:

> The top of Moore's washing machine-sized monument is engraved with the Ten Commandments as excerpted from the Book of Exodus

in the King James Bible. The sides of the monument bear quotations from the Declaration of Independence and smaller quotations from James Madison, William Blackstone, James Wilson, Thomas Jefferson, George Washington and John Jay. Also included in the engravings is the National Motto, "In God We Trust," and quotations excerpted from the 1954 Pledge of Allegiance and the Preamble to the Alabama Constitution. The front of the monument references the Declaration of Independence with the statement, "Laws of Nature and of Nature's God."[55]

Moore again referred to the Declaration in justifying his actions:

> Rights come from God, not from government. If government can give you rights, government can take them away from you. If God gives you rights, no man and no government can take them away from you. That was the premise of the organic law of this country, which is the Declaration of Independence.

So began a battle royal between pro-Mooreites and anti-Mooreites over an engraved block of stone.[56]

I call this debate embarrassing because it is based on a serious misunderstanding of the history of ideas. The "Nature's God" of the Declaration was *not* a Christian god; nor could it have been taken as such by a literate citizen in 1776. Instead, it is a reference to the much vaguer Prime Mover as envisaged by Jefferson, Franklin, Paine, and other freethinkers. Jefferson believed neither in the divinity of Christ nor in the authority of the Bible. By using the idiom "Nature's God," he and his co-signers were, in fact, deliberately distancing themselves from the Christian tradition. Evidence of this abounds. The U.S. treaty with Tripoli (1796–1797) states in so many words that America is not a Christian nation. It was Franklin himself who brought Freemasonry, with its implicit disavowal of Christianity and its reverence for reason and nature, to America in 1735.[57] Washington, Adams, and many other founders were Freemasons, and our own beloved dollar bill is covered with Masonic imagery. Among others of the Founding Fathers who expressed disbelief in the Christian God may be numbered James Madison, Tom Paine, Ethan Allen, and John Adams, and the list of avowed non-Christians also includes Abraham Lincoln.[58]

What makes the Moore issue significant is that there would have been no Moore issue at all if America's press, almost without exception, knew anything about American history.[59] Nothing illustrates our educational poverty or justifies Gore Vidal's phrase "the United States of Amnesia" so aptly as Justice Moore and his treatment by the media.[60] Ignorance of this magnitude can lead to dangerous misunderstandings of law and misuses of power. And ignorance of this magnitude can spring only from an epidemic failure of national education. From the very inception of our democratic system, education was seen as its indispensable underpinning. As Jefferson himself put it,

> I do most anxiously wish to see the highest degrees of education given to the higher degrees of genius, and to all degrees of it, so much as may enable them to read & understand what is going on in the world, and to keep their part of it going on right: for nothing can keep it right but their own vigilant & distrustful superintendence.[61]

Jefferson repeatedly returned to the idea that liberty is viable only if it is protected by an educated electorate, and he put his words into action by helping found and design the University of Virginia.

Leadership and Education. What are the goals of leadership and education in a free society? The Declaration so interestingly cited by Justice Moore describes these goals succinctly:

> We hold these truths to be self-evident, that all men are created equal, that they are endowed by their Creator with certain unalienable Rights, that among these are Life, Liberty and the pursuit of Happiness.—That to secure these rights, Governments are instituted among Men, deriving their just powers from the consent of the governed . . .

Government, then, is instituted to secure "Life, Liberty and the pursuit of Happiness." It does this in three ways. Its military protects us from enemies. Its laws and authorities protect us from itself and from each other. And government even attempts to protect us from ignorance. Aware, as Jefferson was, that life, liberty, and the pursuit of happiness are best enjoyed knowledgeably, leaders at every level of government have helped to institute and maintain a system of universal education. Our schools and colleges, in other words, are not just training camps for the marketplace. They are the staging grounds for liberty.

It is especially urgent for us to remember these foundational and constitutional bases of education. Only an education in liberty can equip Americans to respond to the massive and evolving challenges posed by global leadership, national development, and a vulnerable environment. But most teachers and administrators at the secondary and higher levels seem to have forgotten, if the thought ever occurred to them at all, that they are supposed to be educating for liberty. Consequently, an overwhelming majority of our B.A.'s and B.S.'s are sallying forth into the world as political innocents.

This lack of training is vulgarity at its worst. There is no excess so gross, no abuse so unjust, as popular ignorance of the practice of citizenship. Other ills we can reform or alleviate, but not without a reasoned awareness of our own rights and responsibilities. Citizenship in a free society demands that we be able to tell truth from lie, access and comprehend key information, evaluate new initiatives in terms of history, read critically, and express ourselves coherently. Our education, or lack of education, in these matters ultimately informs our marketplace and selects our leaders. Yet it is precisely this form of education that current curricula ignore.

Higher education has come to this pass through an unfortunate combination of factors. Most colleges cannot afford to staff the sort of writing courses that teach critical thinking and self-expression. Professors, who must publish in specialized fields, have grown more unwilling to teach the sort of lower-division courses that make up a core curriculum. Current academic wisdom tends to dismiss humanities core curricula as arbitrary and outmoded. An opposite agenda, born of leftist wrath and the counterculture of the 1960s, inheres instead. College catalogs and college budgets are crowded with the pedagogy of gender, race, ethnicity, and sexual orientation. Lecture halls buzz with the rhetoric of theorists who dismiss American liberty as subjective and fictional. The discourse of liberty has fallen victim to the free marketry of academe.

The human result of this educational market is a TV viewing public that cannot distinguish, in terms of importance and interest, between the Iraq war and the Laci Peterson case or recognize the corporate cynicism that fueled the reportage of the latter. It is also a consumer public that is excellently informed about what commercial items to buy but dismally ignorant about which ideas of liberty should be loved and preserved.

One might assume from all this that times are good in Vulgarland: that our colleges are finally in sync with our media and our major providers. But this assumption is off the mark. As of the year 2003, only 31 percent of American college graduates were literate enough to perform complex professional tasks.[62] Understandably, employers are no longer satisfied with the B.A. or B.S. Our colleges are not preparing their students for the world. Our standards are too lax. Our curricula are too fragmented. Our faculties are too self-absorbed.

This self-absorption is unintentionally illustrated in a 2003 *ADE* article by Lawrence Schwartz, a professor at Montclair State University. Schwartz claims that, at least on his campus, literary studies are "more alive than ever," and he credits this happy state of affairs to the work of a faculty task force that swept away the old major and brought in a new order of things. The group's 1992 report "made the context of dissatisfaction clear":

> There is the general perception that the structure of the old major no longer meets the challenges of shifting faculty interests, a student constituency undergoing broad sociological change, and an

academic discipline in the midst of dramatic conceptual and institutional transformations.[63]

Schwartz goes on to show how the *new* English major speaks to these considerations by destructuring its requirements, redefining its parameters, and allowing for more curricular variety, all of which tend to make it more "postmodern."

I have no issue with Schwartz's conclusions. "Postmodern," for better or worse, is indeed what the new major is. My question is whether "shifting faculty interests, a student constituency undergoing broad sociological change, and an academic discipline in the midst of dramatic ... transformations" are more important considerations than the basic issue of how much students should know, and what they should be able to do, after completing the English major. We must assume that the English major should be part of a B.A. degree that in some sense prepares students for life in a complex and challenging world. How will altering the major to conform to "shifting faculty interests" contribute to this goal? Here are some of these new interests, as presented by the premier American literary association, the Modern Language Association (MLA):

> The Politics of Critical Language; Cinema; Theory of Literary History; Performance; Literature and the Idea of Europe; Colonialism and the Postcolonial Condition; The Status of Evidence; Ethnicity; Rereading Class; Globalizing Literary Studies; Imagining History; Science Fiction and Literary Studies: The Next Millennium....[64]

A handsome bunch of topics, if you want your paper accepted for the next conference or published in a scholarly journal, but rather recondite when applied to students who have only ten semester courses to learn reading, writing, and critical thinking. Readjusting major requirements to suit this sort of shifting faculty interests would seem both short-sighted and self-serving. And readjusting major requirements to suit *any shifting faculty interests at all* should never be done without the students' best interests in mind. Jonathan Culler more sensibly makes this point in the same *ADE* issue as Schwartz's article:

> If we can imagine a totality of some sort—general education in the humanities, for instance—it will be easier to articulate and argue both the value of the major and what ought to go into it than if we continue to treat it as a conglomeration of the various things we are interested in teaching.[65]

One cannot resist noting that the things professors currently "want to teach"—Critical Language, Cinema, Theory of Literary History, Colonialism and the Post-Colonial Condition, The Status of Evidence, Ethnicity, Class, and Globalization—together with the equally popular topics, Gender and Gay Studies, all have something in common. Though each topic carries its own specific social message, they are all vulgar. They are vulgar in that they ignore, and sometimes seek to obliterate, human continuity: not only the vertical continuity that binds us to all of history, but also the horizontal continuity that binds us to each other. Instead of these continuities, our students are offered sophomoric skepticism and a fragmented world where sects and cadres compete for hegemony. Instead of critical thinking, dons hammer home the politics of interest.

Something similar can be said about changing major requirements to accommodate "a student constituency undergoing broad sociological change." Over the long term, sociological change can contribute to the renewal of professions and the strengthening of institutions. But this observation does not justify short-term accommodations of a major whose goal ought to be political literacy. Academic adjustments in favor of student constituencies, moreover, are often merely ways of asserting political correctness and pandering for enrollment and approval. With motives like these at work, quality always suffers.

Incidentally, "shifting faculty interests" and demographic change have damaged the quality of academic research as well. In our English departments, the staid but accessible research specialties—medieval, Renaissance, eighteenth century, etc.—have been displaced by a hubbub of diverse specialties deriving from ethnicity, race, gender, sexual orientation, political preference, and literary theory. If the old fields were stolid and old-boyish, they nonetheless had the saving grace that it was possible to judge the *quality* of a work or scholar in the light of a "great tradition" of Western letters. Now this practice is all changed. Dozens of new subject areas demand to be judged *in their own light*. Professors who dare to question the validity or relevance of these areas are accused of political incorrectness. Promotion committees, deans, and editors generally lack expertise in these many new fields and are often in a quandary about the quality of specific research and generally (for reasons also connected to political correctness) give candidates the benefit of the doubt. Hence, we now see much published research of a level of quality that would have been dismissed as inadequate by earlier academic generations.

Readers concerned about this state of things might consider asking their local college president the following questions:

Is there something wrong with being able to read and express oneself well?

Is it a sin to be able to tell truth from falsehood?

Does society no longer need an informed and literate populace?

Has citizenship become a meaningless fantasy?

Do young people learn to practice citizenship more or less automatically?

And, if the answers are all no, then follow up with this challenge:

Then why not do something about it?

But what *can* be done? Much can be done, in fact, both in the long term and even in the short term. But before turning to what can be done, let me anticipate two possible misconceptions. First, I would never be able to live with, much less recommend, a college course in citizenship. The topic is too general and, worse, suggests a preachy and vulgar pedagogy. Second, by *discourse of liberty* and *citizenship*, I am not suggesting a flag-waving endorsement of "American" values. Americanisms like complacency, gullibility, materialism, and consumerism are what got education into this mess in the first place.

By *discourse of liberty* and *citizenship,* I mean instead the ability to analyze and critique one's own political system and to reform it if necessary. If the American system is indeed the best in the world, it is so because it is capable of self-criticism and repair. Mere repetition of patriotic mantras is the surest path to failure.

Curricular Reform in the Humanities: A Short-Term Proposal. Because all significant reform requires financing and organization, our college should immediately establish a Task Force for the Humanities or a Project in the Humanities: a committee whose mission is to establish long-term strategies, administer a new program, and raise money. Committee members will be honored and rewarded by being freed of all other committee assignments during their tenure.

During its first year of operation, the task force will be charged with creating a humanities core, spearheaded by an entry-level, full-year humanities course, required for all students. This course should have a regular writing component adequate to confer credit in composition. The course's reading list should be the literature, art, and history of a given historical period. For teaching this course, professors will be rewarded with a renewable, one-course reduction in their instructional load. An example of such a course is offered by Reed College's Humanities 110.[66]

Does our college lack money for developing this core? Money should not be a worry. All the college has to do is reevaluate courses that are already crowding the catalog: courses that thinly veil political agendas, courses that ignore literature in deference to "theory," and courses that support a professor's research ambitions rather than the students' needs. These courses are not liberating our students so much as they are feeding private interests.

Candidates for the B.A. will also be required to take one full year of upper-division history and one full year of upper-division literature from the same historical period. History and literature professors who wish to coordinate their courses with each other will be rewarded with one-time-only instructional relief. This coordination will focus on how exactly the teaching of such courses can enhance a student's self-awareness and social consciousness.

What educational effects would these innovations achieve? They would supply a baseline of humanistic knowledge in all graduates. They would interest students in pursuing a humanities major. Most importantly, they would remind students that the two most important skills for the real world, vulgar opinions to the contrary, are the ability to evaluate information and the ability to express oneself effectively.

Curricular Reform in the Humanities: A Long-Term Strategy. After the humanities core is in place, the task force will turn to the development of a humanities major, not called Humanities per se (again, too broad a term), but rather, in the manner of Harvard College, called History and Literature.[67] This dual concentration has an auspicious pedigree. Rationalism and the Enlightenment, which still inform so many of our institutions, have their roots in Italian humanism, which was based primarily on learnedness in history, literature, and the art of writing. Each student's experience in the dual major will be focused in a tutorial, the instruction of which will be funded by our college's growing endowment for the humanities.

This humanities program will be augmented by coherent long-term infrastructural strategies. The college will use every means to ensure that the humanities program has decent classrooms, office space, and equipment. The endowment will fund an annual lecture series to bring ideas and personalities in from afar. The endowment will offer grants to resident faculty and visiting scholars (a service already in place in many campus humanities centers).

Most importantly, the college will strengthen the humanities and enlarge their scope by *hiring for character*. Too long have colleges' hiring policies been based narrowly on professional expertise— a priority that has led critics to observe that America's colleges are staffed by social misfits. What constitutes character in this context? A zest for scholarship and a hearty love of teaching. A penchant for the life of the mind that transcends gimmicky theories, topical issues, and academic politics. An ability to describe one's research and justify its general significance briefly and clearly. A sense of social responsibility. A distaste for nonsense.

Hiring for character, by the way, can work wonders in *any* field. If we hire for character, we expand the scope of the humanities to enhance every specialty. Even our scientists, linguists, and statisticians will be able to communicate to general audiences and the community at large. And at last our presidents and deans will prize good learning and good teaching.

The Social Goal of Teaching in the Humanities. Even if instituted haphazardly, the Task Force in the Humanities, the humanities core, and the History and Literature major would have a reviving effect on undergraduates. These initiatives are best understood as the academic groundwork for a more socially conscious citizenry. The combination of history and literature, moreover, can be even more effective in expanding a student's social consciousness if it concentrates attention on the expansion of consciousness within an individual period of the past. Reed College describes the first semester of its Humanities 110 as follows:

> The fall semester focuses on the development of culture in ancient Greece, beginning with Homer's *Iliad*. It progresses through the rise and evolution of the *polis* as reflected in the histories of Herodotus and Thucydides as well as in Aeschylus's *Oresteia* and selected plays of Sophocles and other dramatists. The semester ends with the critiques made by Plato and Aristotle in the *Republic* and the *Nicomachean Ethics* of individual and *polis* virtues. Parallel developments in the heroic ideal and civic art are followed through a study of archaic and classical sculpture, vase painting, and architecture. The course concentrates on the Greeks' relation to the gods, to the state, to their fellows, and to their developing self-consciousness.[68]

In the four centuries covered by this course, the ancient Greek mind evolved from polytheistic and preliterate saga to analytic and even utopian thinking, and the Greek idea of politics evolved from tribal rivalries to the Panhellenic empire of Alexander the Great.

These developments vividly suggest the sort of awareness that students should cultivate within themselves. Similar thematics play themselves out in ancient Rome (covered in the second semester of Reed's Humanities 110), Renaissance/Enlightenment Europe, and the United States. Concentration on specific themes within these periods, like religious toleration, civil rights, and women's rights, makes the emphasis on consciousness more pronounced.

Continual attention should be given to the role of fiction, poetry, and drama in enhancing consciousness. In the previous chapter, we saw how Homer manipulates narration and dialogue to bring to our awareness key ideas—new for his time—like shared humanity and individual identity. This technique of using fictional experience to expand awareness is one of the chief means by which enduring art distinguishes itself from its competition. Thus it is through reading "great" books, rather than merely typical books, that students can get the fullest possible experience of past times and the fullest possible expansion of consciousness.

Special Studies in History, Literature, and Consciousness. History, literature, and consciousness do not always interact in terms of simple progress. Some of their interactions have been ironic, even tragic, and instructors should be aware that these negative examples are as essential as the positive ones. In the first place, as consciousness expands in some areas, it contracts in others. I may have read more books than my father's father did, but I will never experience nature as he did as a woodsman in the forests of Russia. Moreover, ideas and principles famous in their own times can be speedily forgotten and hence must be reinvented altogether. Whole paradigms, full of unique vigor and subtlety, can slip out of communal consciousness. One of the marks of great research and teaching in the humanities is the ability to rediscover such neglected paradigms, to reintegrate them and make them live again in class. In such revitalized form, the ideas take on new meaning, not only as vital history, but as alternative instruments for valuation and choice.

Equally important is the study of periods in which consciousness is deliberately limited by an autocratic hierarchy. The execution of Socrates, the persecution of Aristotle, and the banishment of Ovid were all efforts by authority to quell free thought, but these instances pale by comparison with the thousand-year-long gag order on ideas imposed by the Catholic Church and culminating in the so-called Inquisition. Victims of church strictures included Peter Abelard, Marsilius of Padua, Joan of Arc, Desiderius Erasmus, Jan Hus, Giordano Bruno, Galileo Galilei, and, at one point, the whole city of Florence. Modern days have seen equally injurious curbs on consciousness imposed, for example, by Nazi, Communist, and Islamic regimes. And the American educational mass market, with its apparent obliviousness to small points like the creed of our nation's founders, may not be far behind.

The social effects of such tyrannical limitation include a comprehensive degradation of consciousness, affecting the whole spectrum of culture, from economics to religion itself. Afflicted by its own so-called protectors, society stumbles along, at first unwillingly, then unaware that it has any alternative: first enslaved, then vulgarized. It sinks into a moral stupor called *correctness*. Giovanni Boccaccio (1307–1375) diagnosed this condition in Italian society and brought it to the world's attention in his *Decameron*. Here he tells the story of an old man who raises his son in complete solitude, teaching the boy only the ways of the church. Finally, when the boy has grown to young manhood, the father and son must travel to Florence:

> [On the way] they ran into a group of beautiful and elegantly dressed young women who were returning from a wedding feast; when the young man saw them, he immediately asked his father what they were. To this his father replied:
>
> "My son, lower your eyes and do not look, for they are evil."
> Then the son asked, "What are they called?"
> In order not to awaken some potential or anything-but-useful desire in the young man's carnal appetite, the father did not want to tell his son their proper name, that is to say "women," so he answered:

"Those are called goslings."

What an amazing thing to behold! The young man, who had never before seen a single gosling, no longer paid any attention to the palaces, oxen, horses, mules, money, or anything else he had seen, and quickly said:

"Father, I beg you to help me get one of those goslings."

"Alas, my son," said the father, "be quiet; they are evil."

To this the young man replied:

"Are evil things made like that?"

"Yes," his father replied.

And his son answered:

"I do not understand what you are saying or why they are evil. As far as I know, I have never seen anything more beautiful or pleasing than they. They are more beautiful than the painted angels which you have pointed out to me so many times. Oh, if you care for me at all, do what you can to take one of these goslings home with us, and I will take care of feeding it."

His father replied:

"I will not, for you know not how to feed them."

Right then and there, the father sensed that Nature had more power than his intelligence, and he was sorry for having brought his son to Florence.[69]

Boccaccio's tale is so wittily told and so universal in its implications that it can serve as a satiric gloss on thought control in any nation or period. It is a powerful example of how literature can work with history in building social consciousness.

Objections and Response. Some interesting objections can be made to these educational reforms, so why not give them voice?

Your goals are decent enough, you might ask me, but will your humanities core really make a difference out there in the world? Would reading and writing about the ancient Greeks and Romans have helped avert 9/11? Would your charming tale from Boccaccio have affected the outcome of the presidential elections of 2000 and 2004? More generally, would your emphasis on history, literature, and writing draw students into the world rather than (as it does to so many professors) remove them from it?

To all these questions, my stubborn answer is yes. If deans actually hire for character, they will gradually renew the academic marketplace with professors who are energetic, gregarious, direct, and sanguine—everything that today's typical academic is not. Only such teachers, who are themselves capable of facing real-world issues, can convey the real-world significance of history, literature, and writing. And exactly what is this real-world significance? If well taught, history and literature drag us out of our private cubbyholes and into a continuum where all of humanity's dynamic forces function in free play. We come face-to-face with the slow and labored development of political consciousness, the rise of a vigorous city and its fall into complacency, the manifold shapes of dishonesty in pursuit of power, the uses of art for liberation or control, the forces that build or destroy community. We become attentive to the benefits and dangers of society, not only in abstract formulation but also in minute detail. And if we learn these lessons well enough, we go forth into the real world with a spirit at once inquisitive and critical. Our reading of the past has emboldened us to "read" reality: to question the multifarious blandishments of the marketplace, to unpack the meaning of events at large.

That's "liberal" education in the old sense of the word. It liberates because it empowers.

In designing such a curriculum, we cannot overestimate the importance of courses that require writing. The ability to organize thought powerfully and lucidly in writing, important in any period, is quite central to the information age. Good writing is essential in all the major professions and demanded of any individual who wishes to be in serious contact with the world. Students must learn effective writing because knowledge and language are, even more than money itself, the currency of the professional arena. Practice in effective writing helps us think better; it refines our speech; it carries us to the podium. Moreover, when required as part of a humanities core, writing completes the dialogic loop between the lectures, the readings, and the students. Conversely, the shortest route to a nation of barbarians is a generation of college graduates who cannot write. The failure of most colleges to supply this skill is evidenced by the runaway sales of PowerPoint, a software program for thought and presentation.

In summary, higher education ought to be education in liberty. American higher education fails in this regard because it floats rudderless, without a sense of purpose and subject to the push and tug of competing internal interests. Educators need to be reminded from every possible quarter that citizens' ability to think critically, speak and write cogently, and see their own times in historical perspective is the only guarantee of a healthy democracy, and that the only way to ensure this ability is through higher education. No one was aware of these necessities more clearly than Frederick Douglass, one of our most eloquent writers on education. As a young boy, Douglass lived in Baltimore with a Mr. and Mrs. Auld. Mrs. Auld started teaching Douglass to read, only to be reprimanded by her husband:

> "If you give a nigger an inch, he will take an ell. A nigger should know nothing but to obey his master—to do as he is told to do. Learning would spoil the best nigger in the world. Now," said he, "if you teach that nigger (speaking of myself) how to read, there would be no keeping him. It would forever unfit him to be a slave. He would at once become unmanageable, and of no value to his master."[70]

If he were alive today, Frederick Douglass would be gratified at the substantial progress made in civil rights. But he would be alarmed to discover that the very education that liberated him is currently being back-burnered on American campuses. For by denying our students the guarantee of an education in independent thinking, do we not come close to creating a nation of slaves?

CHAPTER NINE

VULGARITY AND CONSCIOUSNESS IN THE NOVEL

If great literature in general provides us with precious means of studying consciousness and renewing it in ourselves, the modern novel deserves special attention. This is because, beginning in the mid-nineteenth century, major novelists began to make consciousness itself a key topic of their narrative proceedings. To these investigative storytellers, it was not just a matter of how much this or that character *knows*, but a subtle interface between a given character's mode of understanding and the world that he or she inhabits. How does a Captain Ahab or an Emma Bovary understand the world at large? What are the consequences of such a worldview? The novelist sets up a dialogue, often ironic or tragic, between individual and social humanity, between innerness and outerness. In appreciating this dialogue, we can learn much about society and ourselves.

This dialogue is usually compounded, in many major novels, with a second form of consciousness: an awareness of the social mores and public circumstances with which individual characters must carry out their dialogues. The history of the novel from Austen and Dickens to the present can be read as a history of modern social consciousness: a vigilance towards injustice, an alertness to vulgarity and flimflam, a concern for the individual in a mass society. Thus, novels can become social documents, as valuable to public policy makers as works of social science or history.

Let us listen to these voices of consciousness at work, particularly with regard to vulgarity, in four novels: *The Great Gatsby, Great Expectations, Madame Bovary,* and *Heart of Darkness.*

Gatsby, Elegance, and Vulgarity. Vulgarity is like quicksand. Our own efforts to escape it tend instead to draw us deeper into it. Consider the amateur grammarians who, seeking elegant speech, banish the use of *me* and *us* as erroneous and produce monstrosities like, "She came along with Richard and I." Or the Jewish immigrants who, eager to assimilate into WASP society, gave their sons Anglo names like Murray, Morris, Stanley, and Irving, only to see these typed as "Jewish" names. Or the prizefighter Cassius Clay, who dropped his "slave name" and dubbed himself Muhammad Ali, without realizing that his new namesake had been a slave trader. It is as though our imitations of culture, if unlit by the lamp of consciousness, entrap us more and more hopelessly in barbarism.

The quicksand runs deeper than this by far. F. Scott Fitzgerald's *Great Gatsby* is the classic rendition of the American Dream: a rhapsody of wealth and style that is rooted in the seemingly magical power of money. Here is Jay Gatsby showing Daisy Buchanan his shirt collection:

> He took out a pile of shirts and began throwing them, one by one, before us, shirts of sheer linen and thick silk and fine flannel, which lost their folds as they fell and covered the table in many-colored disarray. While we admired he brought more and the soft rich heap mounted higher—shirts with stripes and scrolls and plaids in coral and apple-green and lavender and faint orange, and monograms of Indian blue. Suddenly, with a strained sound, Daisy bent her head into the shirts and began to cry stormily.
>
> "They're such beautiful shirts," she sobbed, her voice muffled in the thick folds. "It makes me sad because I've never seen such—such beautiful shirts before."

Daisy is so moved by this pile of shirts that she can barely express herself and must repeat, "I've never seen such—such beautiful shirts before." Gatsby's shirts, each a tangible metaphor for his abundant wealth, assert a spiritual power over her, and she breaks down sobbing. Fitzgerald makes no bones about Gatsby's goals or the source of his charm. His mystique stems from his manipulation of money and his ability to wear his wealth glamorously. But not forever. Gatsby shines briefly, then falls. His friend, narrator Nick Carraway, concludes that this tragedy has occurred, not because Gatsby's dream was unattainable but rather because the dream itself was flawed:

> He had come a long way to this blue lawn, and his dream must have seemed so close that he could hardly fail to grasp it. He did not know that it was already behind him, somewhere back in that vast obscurity beyond the city, where the dark fields of the republic rolled on under the night. . . .
>
> So we beat on, boats against the current, borne back ceaselessly into the past.

Why has the dream failed? Because, Fitzgerald suggests, it based happiness on the raw profit and insensate power that created modern America, in all its glitzy vulgarity. Gatsby, Daisy, and their ilk lack the self-awareness to put this wealth in perspective, and so by implication do most of their fellow Americans.

Evolving Consciousness in *Great Expectations*. *The Great Gatsby* harkens back to another brilliant and evocative novel, Charles Dickens' *Great Expectations*. Philip "Pip" Pirrip, the protagonist and narrator, is born into humble circumstances and put to humble occupations by his uncle and guardian, Joe Gargery; but the boy loathes his status and yearns for something finer:

> I took the opportunity of being alone in the court-yard, to look at my coarse hands and my common boots. My opinion of those accessories was not favourable. They had never troubled me before, but they troubled me now, as vulgar appendages. I determined to ask Joe why he had ever taught me to call those picture-cards, Jacks, which ought to be called knaves. I wished Joe had been rather more genteelly brought up, and then I should have been so too.

Pip is developing, in his own youthful way, a typically British and thoroughly materialistic moral paradigm: a mind-set that automatically confers superiority on the well-to-do and well brought up. But though Dickens gives us every reason to take Pip's feelings seriously, he presents, from very early on, telling evidence opposed to this bourgeois paradigm. This evidence is presented in deft strokes of plot and character. Pip fails to notice that his unlettered uncle and guardian is a man rich in homespun wisdom and benevolence. Unbeknownst to Joe, Pip is pressed into service by Abel Magwitch, an escaped convict. Magwitch is a thoroughly unsavory figure, and when we learn that his wealth is the secret source of Pip's "great expectations" (future inheritance), our feelings about the loot are deeply complicated.

Completing this moral puzzle are Miss Havisham and her niece Estella, who constitute Pip's first brush with the upper class. Pip is amazed to find, on the old lady's dining table, a frightening object that he cannot identify without her help:

> An epergne or centrepiece of some kind was in the middle of this cloth; it was so heavily overhung with cobwebs that its form was quite undistinguishable; and, as I looked along the yellow expanse out of which I remember its seeming to grow, like a black fungus, I saw speckled-legged spiders with blotchy bodies running home to it, and running out from it, as if some circumstances of the greatest public importance had just transpired in the spider community.

The "centrepiece" turns out to be a decayed wedding cake, set out ages past for a groom who never showed up for the wedding. Miss Havisham has turned her dining room into an icon of her own spiritual poverty. For all her breeding and hauteur, she is a traumatized shell of a woman, phobic to good feeling. But Pip, of course, cannot unpack this symbolism. He promptly falls in love with young Estella, a beauty who has inherited both her aunt's aloofness and inability to love. Estella coyly asks Pip for a kiss:

"Come here! You may kiss me, if you like." I kissed her cheek as she turned it to me. I think I would have gone through a great deal to kiss her cheek. But, I felt that the kiss was given to the coarse common boy as a piece of money might have been, and that it was worth nothing.

Hard knocks ultimately cure Pip of his misconceptions and develop his consciousness. He learns to build up his own substance with solid work. He learns to love and respect Joe. He learns that dignity is not to be found in wealth and station, but rather in one's own humbled heart.

Both *The Great Gatsby* and *Great Expectations* can teach us much about the nature of social consciousness, and this lesson can be extended to other socially critical novelists. Social appearances or status symbols are *always* misleading, because they are the means by which the upper classes attempt to compensate for their dissatisfaction and mask their insecurities. Thus, every quality associated with class is doubled by a hidden opposite: wealth–*want,* conviviality–*loneliness,* calm–*anxiety,* love–*disaffection,* pride–*guilt,* and so on. To live without social consciousness is to be trapped in these false appearances and inevitably betrayed by them.

The only alternative to this destruction is the painful transition to awareness. Painful, because consciousness is always alienating and frequently provokes conflict. Nick Carraway must lose his friend Gatsby to achieve his insight about the instability of Gatsby's dream. Pip must see his own dreams broken before he can discover the stark essentials for building a life. Social consciousness is thus the art of cutting through not only the facade of social pretensions, but also the smoke of one's own dreams about social acceptance. Only in the practice of this art can one, like Fitzgerald and Dickens themselves, converse with the unspoken and the unseen.

Fitzgerald and Dickens have yet more to tell us about social consciousness. But not until we add a third discussant to our panel: Gustave Flaubert.

Flaubert and the Challenge of Consciousness. Consciousness is usually offered to the reader for free, indeed as a kind of
enticement, in the form of an intelligent and considerate narrator.
In *The Great Gatsby*, we are shepherded through the sad story by
the bemused and ironic Nick Carraway. In *Great Expectations,* our
traveling companion is Pip, the hero himself, but Pip writing at a
removal in time and with access to new wisdom. These narrators
are not totally unlike the classic third-person narrators of Fielding's
Tom Jones, Thackeray's *Vanity Fair,* or Dickens' own *Bleak House*:
The narrations are so constructed as to seem to focus on the action
through a window of rationality. Not so Gustave Flaubert in his
masterpiece, *Madame Bovary*. Flaubert's narration is impersonal,
downbeat, almost sterile. There are no conclusions drawn, no con-
fidences offered. The reader is denied the solace of companionship
and the security of counsel.

Add to this that Flaubert's innovative technique also denies us
the orientation of a general introduction or conclusion. The novel
begins with a deadpan schoolroom vignette:

> We were in class when the head-master came in, followed by a "new
> fellow," not wearing the school uniform, and a school servant carry-
> ing a large desk. Those who had been asleep woke up, and every one
> rose as if just surprised at his work.[71]

It ends with even more deadpan gossip about the success and honors won by a thoroughgoing cad and opportunist:

> Since Bovary's death three doctors have followed one another at
> Yonville without any success, so severely did Homais attack them.
> He has an enormous practice; the authorities treat him with con-
> sideration, and public opinion protects him.
>
> He has just received the cross of the Legion of Honour.

It is as though a camera and mike had turned on automatically at one
moment of history and off again at another. This bareness of style
gives us the sense of reportage, of firsthand reality, of uncomfort-

able intimacy. The narrative speaks to us as if it was of such awful clarity that it needs no assistance or advertisement from its author. Yet, in so doing, it challenges us to draw our own conclusions about the events and characters portrayed.

Flaubert's subject matter is initially uninspiring. We meet the protagonist, Emma Rouault, through the limited awareness of the provincial doctor, Charles Bovary. Almost immediately, Charles conceives of her as an erotic object:

> So she went to fetch a bottle of curacao from the cupboard, reached down two small glasses, filled one to the brim, poured scarcely anything into the other, and, after having clinked glasses, carried hers to her mouth. As it was almost empty she bent back to drink, her head thrown back, her lips pouting, her neck on the strain. She laughed at getting none of it, while with the tip of her tongue passing between her small teeth she licked drop by drop the bottom of her glass.

But after Emma marries Charles, Flaubert takes us beyond Charles' perceptions and into the inner world of his wife's aspirations. First the author conveys Emma's yearning for romantic love and her secret feeling that genuine romance is impossible without exotic locations and effects. Would that she had been

> in post chaises behind blue silken curtains to ride slowly up steep roads, listening to the song of the postilion re-echoed by the mountains, along with the bells of goats and the muffled sound of a waterfall; at sunset on the shores of gulfs to breathe in the perfume of lemon trees; then in the evening on the villa-terraces above, hand in hand to look at the stars, . . . Why could not she lean over balconies in Swiss chalets, or enshrine her melancholy in a Scotch cottage, with a husband dressed in a black velvet coat with long tails, and thin shoes, a pointed hat and frills?

Emma is a dreamer, but her dreams are not of real adventure or self-discovery; rather they savor of the romanticized quick fixes—post-chaises, Swiss chalets, Scotch cottages—that populate cheap fiction. Her loving husband seems vulgar to her:

> Charles's conversation was commonplace as a street pavement, and everyone's ideas trooped through it in their everyday garb, without exciting emotion, laughter, or thought. . . . A man, on the contrary, should he not know everything, excel in manifold activities, initiate you into the energies of passion, the refinements of life, all mysteries? But this one taught nothing, knew nothing, wished nothing.

Is Flaubert making Emma a missionary of consciousness? So it would seem, from her disgruntled read on her own provincial environment. It turns out, however, that Flaubert is just doubling the satiric ante. A dreamer may well transcend provincial vulgarity, but not, Flaubert suggests, if she herself has vulgar dreams.

Emma's dreams are vulgar not only because (like Gatsby's) they are based on popular misconceptions, but also because (like Pip's) they envisage a happiness gained without spiritual investment. Her yearning for a man who will "know everything, excel in manifold activities, initiate you into the energies of passion, the refinements of life, all mysteries" is, above all, that opiate of the popular ignorance, the craving for a free ride. This craving leads her into the infidelities and financial blunders that in the end destroy her.

Flaubert leaves the world of *Madame Bovary* a closed circle of stunted awareness, an arena in which various sects of vulgarity (like Matthew Arnold's "ignorant armies" who "clash by night") compete with each other for eminence.

Fitzgerald, Dickens, and Flaubert give us three different impressions regarding the extent and quality of consciousness. In *The Great Gatsby*, Nick Carraway's conclusion that, in spite of our best efforts, we are all "borne back ceaselessly into the past," is tempered by the fact that he has neither followed Gatsby's example nor been implicated in Gatsby's fall. On the other hand, his words *do* imply that as Americans we are all cursed with a "dream" that founders in its own materialism. The implication, then, is that being an American has its moral hazards: a serious but not wholly damning injunction. Yet those who know something about his creator's biography might also wonder if Nick is not conveying an intimation from the author.

Fitzgerald was notorious for his own glimmer and glitter. Is Fitzgerald intimating to us that, as an American, even *he* may be denied the transfiguring consciousness that will save him from himself?

In *Great Expectations,* the read on consciousness is yet more problematic, because the author himself waffled regarding his final message. Dickens' view, as presented above, is that the only alternative to spiritual destruction is the painful transition to awareness. But exactly *how* painful? Quite painful indeed, implied Dickens' first edition of the novel. Here Pip, self-redeemed and self-enfranchised, must yet face lifelong alienation from his beloved Estella. This was a powerful conclusion, true to life and conveying the sad fact that consciousness, though liberating, tends to separate us from the communal hearth. But Dickens was convinced by a friend that this ending was too dark. Pip should have his reward; Estella too should be redeemed. Dickens followed this rather crowd-pleasing advice and wrote a second conclusion. In so doing, he significantly vulgarized his novel, making it weak in the precise area of its earlier strength.

Flaubert handles consciousness the most subtly of the three novelists. By denying us the convenience of a personal narrator or the stability of a general opening or conclusion, he throws the ball into our court. We the readers are challenged to supply the novel's "consciousness": its scorn or compassion or indifference, its perspective, its sense of right and wrong. We must complete the author's deliberately unfinished world. We must, as best we can, explain the forces, psychological and social, that drive Emma to her own destruction. And once we have done that, we may address the bigger and more oppressive question of whether our own society, indeed any society, no matter how sophisticated, is not silently enslaved by vulgarities of its own. After all, didn't Gustave Flaubert himself, in answer to a question about his heroine, say, *"Emma Bovary, c'est moi"*?

Consciousness As Curse and Salvation: Joseph Conrad. After completing his horrific navigation in Africa, Charles Marlow, sea captain, moralist, and Joseph Conrad's favorite narrator, returns to the tidy European city that he calls the "whited sepulcher" and is appalled by the vulgarity of its citizens:

> I found myself back in the sepulchral city resenting the sight of people hurrying through the streets to filch a little money from each other, to devour their infamous cookery, to gulp their unwholesome beer, to dream their insignificant and silly dreams. They trespassed upon my thoughts.

These feelings are new to Marlow, because he is no longer the man he was. In Africa he has met the famous Kurtz, a European champion of "enlightenment" who has in fact been completely corrupted by his absolute power over the natives. Through Kurtz, Marlow has become aware of a "horror": a curse inhering not only in African natives and the great colonial powers, but also—to Marlow—in human nature itself. This horror is an intimation of appalling inhumanity and a prophecy of future disaster.

As Marlow's consciousness is painful, so is it alienating. He can share it only with those whom he deems capable of enduring it. At the novel's end, face-to-face with the grieving former fiancée of the now-deceased Kurtz, he cannot tell the truth about Kurtz's last words ("The horror! the horror!"):

> I was on the point of crying at her, "Don't you hear them?" The dusk was repeating them in a persistent whisper all around us, in a whisper that seemed to swell menacingly like the first whisper of a rising wind. "The horror! the horror!"
>
> "His last word—to live with," she murmured. "Don't you understand I loved him—I loved him—I loved him!"
>
> I pulled myself together and spoke slowly.
>
> "The last word he pronounced was—your name."

For Marlow, consciousness of "the horror" is like a guilty secret. But unlike Kurtz, he is not destroyed by his own consciousness. Having seen but not tasted the horror, he may survive:

True, he [Kurtz] had made that last stride, he had stepped over the edge, while I had been permitted to draw back my hesitating foot. And his consciousness, terrifying and incriminating as it is, nonetheless carries a form of redemption. To understand exactly why, we must move backwards from the novel's conclusion and into its heart, which is also the heart of the jungle. There, in a hut built of reeds by the river, Marlow discovers an old book about seamanship:

> Within, Towson or Towser [the book's author] was inquiring earnestly into the breaking strain of ships' chains and tackle, and other such matters. Not a very enthralling book; but at the first glance you could see there *a singleness of intention, an honest concern for the right way of going to work, which made these humble pages, thought out so many years ago, luminous with another than a professional light. The simple old sailor, with his talk of chains and purchases, made me forget the jungle and the pilgrims in a delicious sensation of having come upon something unmistakably real.* (italics added)

What redeems Marlow is not merely his consciousness of the truth, or even his chivalric suppression of it. It is both of these combined with his commitment to "a singleness of intention, an honest concern for the right way of going to work." It is the ability to hold unsettling truth in mind but still to concentrate on what is immediate and honest and possible. This is what enables human wholeness, what produces something "unmistakably real."

The Triumph and Tragedy of Consciousness. Fitzgerald, Dickens, Flaubert, and Conrad, though differing in tone, are essentially all of a piece. Each of the four novels is, in its own way, an assertion of consciousness in the face of popular ignorance. Thus, vulgarity is a theme in each novel, whether it is mentioned by name or not. Similar thematics appear in other major writers in both fiction and nonfiction, including Austen, Thoreau, Tolstoy, Dostoevsky, Melville, Arnold, Joyce, Kafka, Mann, Forster, Hesse, de Beauvoir, Lampedusa, and Chandler.[72] None of these was a coterie writer; most were widely read in their own time. What they sought to resist, however, was a truly pandemic phenomenon: the swelling mass markets and mass cultures of Europe and America. These markets and cultures produced a uniquely dangerous kind of vulgarity—vulgarity that was institutionalized and proper, vulgarity that could be elected to public office, vulgarity that could characterize a new and barbaric ruling class. There was no antidote for this poison except consciousness: specifically, consciousness of the spiritual poverty and political instability of mass culture; more generally, consciousness of concepts that have positive value across time and space.

It did not matter that consciousness could not command armored divisions, or that, as Dostoevsky noted, consciousness could be at times more paralyzing than ignorance. What mattered was that consciousness was a seed that might grow stronger in some future time. Consciousness thus became, for all its alienation and malaise, the closest thing to an intellectual religion. It is thanks in part to this stubbornly preserved conviction that our current society retains a measure of self-awareness.

Yet as with all powerful faculties, consciousness is heady stuff, dangerous in strong doses and conspicuously liable to misuse. The disciplined and chivalric consciousness endorsed by Conrad in *Heart of Darkness* was lost on many younger writers, who would launch arbitrary and ruthless attacks on the "masses." H. G. Wells, D. H. Lawrence, George Bernard Shaw, Virginia Woolf, and Wyndham Lewis took part in these diatribes, as did, more poetically, T. S. Eliot and Ezra Pound. In *The Intellectuals and the Masses,* John Carey quotes Friedrich Nietzsche, the intellectual godfather of this movement, who maintained that "the great majority of men have no right to existence, but are a misfortune to higher men." Nietzsche, Lawrence, and Eliot wished to deny the majority any literate education at all:

> "Let all schools be closed at once," he [Lawrence] exhorts. "The great mass of humanity should never learn to read or write." . . .

Without education the masses will, Lawrence hopes, relapse into purely physical life. . . . In this way the dangers of a "presumptuous, newspaper-reading population may be averted."[73]

Sentiments of this sort make it clear that Lawrence, Eliot, and others saw themselves as part of a besieged power base—that not only their security but also their very means of thinking were threatened by pulp-schooled hordes. The stand they took reads suspiciously like the aristocratic arrogance and intolerance of the European past. But their poison spread into other social venues as well. Programmatic misanthropy of exactly this sort would also surface in the manifestos of that crowd-pleasing demagogue, Adolf Hitler, who would whip Germany into a chauvinist frenzy and, in the bargain, realize Conrad's prophecy of horror.[74]

What does the Nietzschean phenomenon suggest about consciousness and vulgarity? Nietzsche, Lawrence, and Eliot had consciousness to spare, but they machined their consciousness into adversarial ideology. Driven by fear and loathing, they debased their most precious faculty into a weapon of interest. Thus debased, their consciousness no longer functioned as a focus for inquiry but became instead a rhetorical implement. To remain effective, consciousness of anyone or anything must be tempered by a presiding *self*-consciousness that adds perspective and militates against bias and excess. You can be as clever as Friedrich Nietzsche, but without self-awareness, your ivory tower will become a breeding-house for fools.

A Footnote on Advanced Vulgarity

Gatsby, Pip, Emma, and Kurtz are all examples of what might be termed a vulgarity of ideas. None of these four figures is a producer or consumer of the mass market, but each of them derives from a mass market of popular gestalts. Gatsby and Pip build their ideologies on the idea of wealth; Emma builds hers on popularized romanticism; Kurtz builds his on enlightenment itself. None of these figures, at least at first, questions these ideas: The ideas are accepted, unconditionally, as a proper cultural inheritance. Each idea has its own energy, its social élan, driving the character into action. But each idea also has its own special blindness, leading each character to a crisis that results either in tragedy or in new consciousness.

Vulgarity, then, inheres in being the puppet of culture. Think of Huck Finn's dad, whose redneck culture blames everything on the "guvment." Think of Captain Ahab, whose Protestant culture impels him to destroy a force of nature. Then think of the American media, where almost every spoken or written opinion suggests some form of mass-produced point of view.

You may object that all major ideas are, in effect, mass-produced. With a few reservations, I would agree. But the ability to question them is not. And it is for the gift of this ability that we have, in large measure, the modern novel to thank.

CHAPTER TEN

THE NATURE OF SOCIAL CONSCIOUSNESS

The Douglass Paradigm and the Birth of Social Consciousness

How is social consciousness born in the real world? Listen again to Frederick Douglass describing the birth of his own awareness in the company of that unthinkable vulgarian, Mr. Auld:

> "Now," said he, "if you teach that nigger (speaking of myself) how to read, there would be no keeping him. It would forever unfit him to be a slave. He would at once become unmanageable, and of no value to his master. As to himself, it could do him no good, but a great deal of harm. It would make him discontented and unhappy." These words sank deep into my heart, stirred up sentiments within that lay slumbering, and called into existence an entirely new train of thought. It was a new and special revelation, explaining dark and mysterious things, with which my youthful understanding had struggled, but struggled in vain. I now understood what had been to me a most perplexing difficulty—to wit, the white man's power to enslave the black man. . . . Though conscious of the difficulty of learning without a teacher, I set out with high hope, and a fixed purpose, at whatever cost of trouble, to learn how to read.

Douglass' narration of his awakening consciousness beats any theoretical interpretation of this process that I have read. Douglass speaks of consciousness as an event involving the whole human being: thought, memory, emotion, personality, experience, social interaction. Its classic succinctness can speak out to all time.

Let us experience this phenomenon in stages. In Douglass' case, the first stage of social consciousness is suffering. Douglass is young, enslaved, and alone. The kindly Mrs. Auld tries to teach him literacy, but Mr. Auld, who is Douglass' lord and master, cuts off this act of humanity, adding a heartless putdown about what "niggers" ought and ought not to learn. Often, suffering can be a mind-numbing thing, but in this case, it comes suddenly and at the perfect moment to create a learning experience. Suffering "stirred up sentiments within that lay slumbering, and called into existence an entirely new train of thought."

The second stage of social consciousness is the recognition of injustice. This comes from Douglass' simple act of ascribing his suffering to a human cause and a specific agency: "I now understood what had been to me a most perplexing difficulty—to wit, the white man's power to enslave the black man." White men were keeping black men down by not allowing them the very education that would enable them to demand a better life. Enslavement is not a law of nature, not even a fact of life. Enslavement is a personal injustice.

The third stage of social consciousness is a sense of empowerment. Once Douglass realizes that his suffering is the result of an injustice visited upon him in specific ways, he is doubly empowered: first by the sudden image of hard facts previously hidden; second, by the sense that injustice applied in specific ways can be reversed in equally specific ways. As Douglass puts it later in the same passage, "Though conscious of the difficulty of learning without a teacher, I set out with high hope, and a fixed purpose, at whatever cost of trouble, to learn how to read." Since injustice is not a natural but a human thing, it can be humanly reversed. Douglass seizes on this truth and is empowered by it.

The final stage of social consciousness and self-empowerment is the perception of ignorance or vulgarity. Douglass follows Auld's reasoning faithfully, but realizes, as Auld does not, that it can be turned upside-down:

> The very decided manner with which he spoke, and strove to impress his wife with the evil consequences of giving me instruction, served to convince me that he was deeply sensible of the truths he was

uttering. It gave me the best assurance that I might rely with the utmost confidence on the results which, he said, would flow from teaching me to read. What he most dreaded, that I most desired. What he most loved, that I most hated.

The consciousness of injustice is almost always connected with a consciousness of ignorance: either the ignorance of the victim or the ignorance of the offender or both. From Auld's perspective, slaves are ignorant and will remain "good" slaves only as long as this ignorance is enforced. Thus Douglass recognizes not only his own ignorance as an unlettered slave, but also the ignorance of Auld, who complacently gives up what will undo his own class: the secret that will free Douglass and other slaves. Auld's brand of ignorance and vulgarity is common among the perpetrators and beneficiaries of injustice. It rests in the illusion that one can treat people obscenely and keep them unaware of it.

Looking at the forms of American injustice and vulgarity that have been treated on these pages, we note again and again that the Douglass Paradigm holds true. Whether the perpetrator is a tobacco company, a cable news channel, a housing developer, or an oil company, the four-stage model operates in terms of social response. The principal job of the vulgarizer is to keep victims unaware that they *are* victims: to characterize a cigarette as "a treat instead of a treatment," a provocation to voyeurism as essential news, an ecological disaster as a "ranch," a gallon of gas as a bargain. Empowerment to combat these vulgarities comes from education: schooling not only in specific terms of this or that evil, but also in general terms of the human condition.

Social Consciousness As Memory

To what extent are we temporal vulgarians? My father, who was born in 1912, spent much of his childhood in the company of a freed slave. When I was born in 1938, many thousands of emancipated slaves were still alive. Yet there has been time enough for many Texans to forget that Texas fought two wars in defense of slavery, and time enough to glorify the site of one of these wars (see Chapter 3). History is powerful stuff, so powerful that people will do anything to forget it.

A few nasty items concerning slavery suggest our discomfort with history: Abraham Lincoln waffled in his strategy regarding blacks, at one point opining that they might be better off back in Africa. John Wilkes Booth, on the other hand, felt that slavery in the United States was a fairer deal for black people than repatriation in Africa. As Booth perhaps knew, slavery was alive and well in Africa, and many slaveholders were themselves black. Not all Northerners, by any means, were against slavery, and many who *were* antislavery held this position not because they thought slavery unjust, but rather because they did not want an influx of blacks in their communities. Native Americans held large numbers of slaves.[75] Walt Whitman's maternal grandparents held slaves at their farm on Long Island. Finally, not only Thomas Jefferson was a slaveholder, but also other Founding Fathers, including George Washington, who willed his slaves their liberty, but stipulated that this manumission should occur only after the death of his wife, Martha. These embarrassing circumstances are far from being common knowledge in American culture.

An example of more systematic historical censorship can be found in the city of Florence in the middle of the fifteenth century. Since the beginning of the fourteenth century, Florence had had poor to awful relations with the papal see, whose policies the city found oppressive, and in 1375, under the chancellorship of the famous humanist Collucio Salutati (1331–1406), Florentine sentiment against the pope boiled over. Salutati's motto, and the battle-cry of the Florentine commune, was "Liberty." A fundraising council of eight citizens (popularly called the Eight Saints) was set up, troops were marshaled, and hostilities were commenced. The inconclusive War of the Eight Saints went on for three years.

Salutati's successor as chancellor was another well-known

scholar, Leonardo Bruni (1370–1444). A mere child during the War of the Eight Saints, Bruni later came to believe that the war had been a great embarrassment for the city of Florence. He decided to take measures. When, in the last year of his life, he published his history of Florence, the account had laundered out the war's most interesting and controversial features, including the Florentines' use of the word *liberty*. Bruni's work was influential—so influential that five and a half centuries later, historians are still sorting out the real events of the 1370s.[76]

Bruni probably acted with the best of intentions. But in censoring the history of the War of the Eight Saints, he robbed future Florentines of the memory of how extensively their city had defied an oppressive regime. The loss of this precious memory must have influenced Florentine policy and culture in the decades that followed. Bruni's act had broader implications as well. In hushing up an unsightly war, he deprived the world of the awareness that, for perhaps the first time in history, a single state had defied an international power in the name of liberty.

These examples all point to the magical—sometimes even demonic—power of history in culture. The past, which created the present, and thus to some extent seems to control the present, is often regarded as some dark, brooding force, some ghostly forebear retaining the power to shame and damn. As though in self-defense, individuals take measures to tame the past, disable its threats, cleanse it of embarrassment, resolve its sleepless ambiguities. Yet these revisions and abridgements can only impoverish and vulgarize the present, for time is very much like space. Our success, and sometimes even our survival, depend on our ability to distinguish the landmarks and perils of the past, perhaps availing ourselves of a rare opportunity to build ourselves, in the light of earlier experience, new and more enlightened institutions.

As our only knowable pathway through time, the past is our birthright and our responsibility. Historical perspective is the benchmark of social consciousness. Additionally, the past is a vital component in basic thinking, as psychologist Donald Norman remarks in *The Design of Everyday Things*:

> Thought and memory are closely related, for thought relies heavily upon the experiences of life. Indeed, much problem solving and decision making take place through attempts to remember some previous experience that can serve as a guide for the present.[77]

Memory is a critical problem-solving tool. When faced with some momentous issue, people tend less to conduct point-by-point analyses than simply to consult their memories. How have I faced similar issues in the past? What have been the ablest historical responses to this issue? The War of the Eight Saints was used in precisely this way by the English reformer John Wycliff (1330–1385) when he opposed papal authority, and through Wycliff, the war also influenced the Czech reformer Jan Hus.[78] But, thanks to Bruni, it would not be used by many others.

The passion for shared memory is nowhere illustrated more abundantly than in the journals of the scholar and teacher Victor Klemperer (1881–1960). A German Protestant of Jewish descent, Klemperer was ostracized, humiliated, robbed of his home, and ultimately marked for extermination by the Nazis. Ironically, the Allied bombing of February 13, 1945, which devastated his home city of Dresden, gave him and his wife, Eva, a chance to escape. Although in their sixties and in poor health, they managed to reach British occupation forces in Bavaria and to survive the war.

The voluminous Klemperer journals deal with politics, scholarship, personal relationships, personal health, and private opinions. But a subject that increases in importance for him as the years pass is the Nazis' slyly nuanced persecution of the Jews. Klemperer unflinchingly recounts the gradually escalating cruelties—compulsory possession of a "Jewish card," compulsory display of a sewn-on yellow Star of David, restrictions on food and travel, forced labor, arrests, house searches, and, ultimately, deportations.

He first has suspicions, and then is convinced, that Auschwitz and other concentration camps are sites of mass murder. He begins to write secretly and hide his journal pages in a large Greek dictionary, knowing that their discovery by the Nazis would spell death for him. On May 27, 1942, he resolves to make his journal a testimony to the future:

> This afternoon Eva is going to Pirna to fetch some money. I shall give her the diary pages of the last few weeks to take with her. After the house search [May 23] I found several books, which had been taken off the shelf, lying on the desk. If one of them had been the Greek dictionary, if the manuscript pages had fallen out and thus aroused suspicion, it would have meant my death. One is murdered for lesser misdemeanors. [. . .] So these parts will go today. But I shall go on writing. That is *my* heroism. I will bear witness, precise witness![79]

Klemperer is precise indeed. In July 1941, he grimly details his eight days of imprisonment in Cell 89, occasioned by a minor blackout violation. In May 1942, a new law forbidding Jews to own pets forces the Klemperers to euthanize Muschel the cat:

> May 19, Tuesday toward evening
> Eva had already made inquiries last week. . . . We hesitated for days. Today news came that a handover order was on its way from the Community, after reception of which I would no longer have the right to dispose of the animal as I saw fit. . . . I left the decision to Eva. She took the animal away in the familiar cardboard cat box, she was present when he was put to sleep by an anaesthetic that took effect very rapidly—the animal did not suffer. But *she* suffers.

Klemperer then unceremoniously details the rest of his day:

> With bad pains in my throat I lugged up 30 pounds of potatoes from our van trader on Wasaplatz. There the man already had my card in his hand, when a young female, dyed-blonde hair, dangerously narrow-minded-looking face, perhaps a shopkeeper's wife, stepped up from behind: "I was here first—the Jew has to wait." Jensch

served her obediently, and the Jew waited. Now it is almost seven o'clock, and the Jew is again waiting for the house search (which usually takes place in the evening).[80]

The night of February 13, 1945, brings the destruction of Dresden by Allied bombs, and the Klemperers are caught in the middle of it. As they try to reach an air-raid shelter, bombs fall around them:

> Eva was two steps ahead of me. We came to the entrance hall of No. 3. At that moment a big explosion nearby. I kneeled, pressing myself against the wall, close to the courtyard door. When I looked up, Eva had disappeared, I thought she was in our cellar. It was quiet, I ran across the yard to our Jews' cellar. A group of people cowered whimpering to the right of the door, I kneeled on the left, close to the window. I called out several times to Eva. No reply. Big explosions. Again the window on the wall opposite burst open, again it was bright as day, again water was pumped. Then an explosion at the window close to me. Something hard and glowing hot struck the right side of my face. I put my hand up, it was covered in blood, I felt for my eye, it was still there.[81]

If there is an opposite to Leonardo Bruni, it is Victor Klemperer. For Bruni, history is a text amenable to censorship. For Klemperer, history is a sacred thing and preserving its every detail an act of faith. Klemperer does not bother us with moralisms. His frankness is morality pure and simple. And, much like that of Frederick Douglass, Klemperer's sense of history is a consciousness that emanates from the full character and extends through all the details of life. Telling the whole story in human detail is the only way to create shared memory.

Social Consciousness in Action

Frederick Douglass has taught us something about how social consciousness is born. Victor Klemperer has shown how social consciousness relates to the past and present. Now let us look at social consciousness in action. To me, the process boils down to four ideas:

Social consciousness addresses issues.
Social consciousness appreciates continuities.
Social consciousness maintains perspective.
Social consciousness incorporates self-awareness.

These ideas can be fleshed out in terms of some familiar material.

Social Consciousness Addresses Issues. In Chapter 3 we visited the Pentagon, where two officials spoke of "the possibility that political life may be closely linked to deception." This policy toward fact and fiction was presumably at work in President George W. Bush's 2003 State of the Union address, in which he boldly described Iraqi "weapons of mass destruction" (WMD) without having dependable evidence that any of these weapons existed. By the summer of that year, the president's comments had become a cause célèbre. Had our commander in chief been *lying*? The behavior of the White House and the press in the two years that followed became an object lesson in social consciousness or want of same. The White House, loath to treat the issue openly, denied that there was any issue at all.[82] The buck was passed to the CIA, whose director, after a pregnant pause, dutifully resigned. Bob Woodward, the senior reporter who arguably had the best access to administration sources, withheld pertinent information as a means of optimizing his own position. The D.C. press corps peevishly flogged the WMD issue for months, mysteriously ignoring the much more serious question of *why* a commander in chief would stretch the facts to justify a war. Was this second issue simply too hot to handle?

In the months following the invasion, only one journalist attempted to address both issues squarely. In the *New York Times* of August 3, 2003, Middle East expert Thomas Friedman summarized British Prime Minister Tony Blair's beliefs about the Iraqi situation:

> Removing Saddam and building a more decent Iraq would help tilt the Middle East onto a more progressive political track and send a message to all the neighboring regimes that Western governments were not going to just sit back and let them incubate suicide

bombers and religious totalitarians, whose fanaticism threatened all open societies. These were the good reasons for the war, and Mr. Blair voiced some of them aloud that day.

The United States had a "master plan" behind its aggression against Iraq. This plan was global and ambitious, and it made a kind of risky sense. Why then didn't Bush come clean about it? Because, according to Friedman, it was a "war of choice," and democracies like America and the U.K. prefer "wars of necessity." Bush and Blair decided to spin a war of the first type as a war of the second type:

> So what Mr. Blair (and Mr. Bush) did was to make a war of choice — but a good choice — into a war of necessity. Because people in democracies don't like to fight wars of choice. To make it a war of necessity, they hyped the direct threat from Iraq and highlighted flimsy intelligence suggesting that Saddam was not just a potential problem, but an immediate, undeterrable threat to the British and American mainlands. This was so, they argued, because Saddam retained hidden stocks of WMDs, in violation of U.N. resolutions, which he could deploy at any minute.[83]

Friedman's interpretation of U.S. policy may be called a fair-to-middling example of social consciousness. In a journalistic arena in which his colleagues were either supporting administration policies or grumbling about rhetoric, Friedman faced the issue as best he could, and put the moose on the table.

Unfortunately, however, not the whole moose. Friedman ignores the dark side of WMD. He ignores the influence of Big Oil on Bush policy in Iraq. He ignores the likely possibility that Bush & Co. waged war as a means of distracting the country and solidifying their own electoral base. Finally, he admits the dishonesty of the Bush rhetoric but ignores its arrogance. For Bush to characterize the questionable as actual and to lead citizens to war without revealing his underlying motives suggests that the president and his team held the intelligence of the American people, as well as Congress and the press, in low esteem. So does a subsequent administration gloss on the subject, Press Secretary's Ari Fleischer's press briefing of July 14, 2003:

> Ari Fleischer conveyed the Bush team's general contempt for the media's interest in the Niger "documents" [a false lead about WMDs used as real by Bush], and, more generally, for the fact that, three months after the fall of Baghdad, Saddam Hussein's arsenal so far appears more chimerical than chemical. "The President has moved on," Fleischer said. . . . "And I think, frankly, much of the country has moved on as well." The very idea that the Administration had put Iraq's nuclear ambitions at the center of its case for war, Fleischer said, was, "a bunch of bull."[84]

Note the repeated euphemism, "moved on," which can mean either "progressed beyond" or "evaded" the issue of presidential honesty. Note also the coarse idiom, "a bunch of bull." How does this expletive get us nearer to the truth? The intention seems to have been to stun and intimidate rather than to enlighten. In using words and phrases of this sort, Fleischer and his employers showed disrespect for the press and the public, who, complacent as they might be, could not be expected to swallow institutional obfuscation forever. By late 2005, thanks to a special investigation into the outing of a CIA operative, the Bush-Cheney machinations with respect to invading Iraq would be hung out to dry.

These phenomena suggest overall that, in its coverage of Bush war policy from 2003 to 2005, the U.S. press was not maintaining a respectable level of social consciousness. And if we ask why not, a little huddle of regime-friendly journalistic attitudes presents itself: unwillingness to startle a nation at war. Corporate interests in control of the media. Complacency and gullibility. Respect for power. Fear of rocking the boat. It is on such attitudes that the Bushes and Cheneys of the world grow fat.

Social Consciousness Appreciates Continuities. Of course, Thomas Friedman could not have faced the Bush-Blair honesty issue at all without an awareness of broader continuities, in terms of the socioeconomic history of the Middle East and the shared memory of the effects of earlier U.S. policies in that region. A sense of historical continuity, not only in terms of past events but in terms of enduring issues, imparts moral substance and sense of direction. Victor Klemperer addresses one of these continuities without missing a beat in his narration. Before entering Cell 89 in the Dresden jail, he was forced by the authorities to remove his belt. In the days that followed, his slipping trousers became symbolic:

> My trousers are slipping, my trousers are slipping. What good is all philosophizing about the inviolability of one's inner moral dignity? I experienced the misery of the slipping trousers, then of the tied-up trousers, as the most extreme humiliation. And I did not remove my collar, even when it was very hot, because that gave me something at least to hold on to.[85]

The continuity here is the idea of human dignity. Klemperer's slipping trousers symbolize both a man's desire for the humble dignity of proper dress and the dismissal of this and all other dignities by a tyrannical government. Klemperer is a master of realistic detail, and this skill allows him to drive home the consciousness of his own humanity, and the inhumanity of others, in a few concise sentences.

Social Consciousness Maintains Perspective. Perspective is to space what continuity is to time. The gatekeepers of closed paradigms, be they American slaveholders, Nazis, or Soviets, take every opportunity to deny their victims perspective: access to the information from the outer world that will bring consciousness. But fortunately, the information prisons are drafty places, haunted by sounds and light from outside. Can states retain systems where ethnic groups, races, even whole genders, are denied basic civil rights? Only, I imagine, if all rationality is banished and victims more or less unanimously support their oppressors. Only under such conditions can people suffer that most extreme of deprivations, the loss of perspective.

The reader may imagine that this is a reference to the Middle

Eastern states that are under the sway of fundamentalist Islam. But these are cases so obvious as to need no documentation. The paradigm prisons to be discussed here are solidly Western. They come in two varieties: the pious prison and the plastic prison.

Pious prisons grow up around religious authority and public fear. The Plymouth settlement of 1620, which would ultimately play a major part in the foundation of a new American nation, was an escape from the pious prison of the Church of England. A century and a half later, the founders took pains decisively to separate church from state. But even today, religion can be used to control and to inhibit. George W. Bush made a profession of Christian faith one of the bases of his 2004 presidential campaign. In so doing, he forced his opponent, John Kerry, into a rhetorical bind. Should Kerry tell it like it was, refer to the separation of church and state, draw a line in the sand between reason and faith, and accuse Bush of Bible-toting demagoguery? Should he have averred, to Bush and to the nation at large, that religious belief should never be a decisive factor in a rational society, since religious belief is subjective, divisive, arbitrary, and beyond appeal? A bold move, and probably well worth the risk. Instead, the overcautious Kerry fell into line behind Bush as a man of faith: a concession that probably did him no good at all in the election. From a tactical perspective, the Bush team fettered their opponent with Christian handcuffs.

More brutal examples are available. Here is Mary Gordon reviewing a 2002 movie about the Magdalene Asylums in Ireland:

> "The Magdalene Sisters," by the Scottish director Peter Mullan, . . . is a fictional rendering of a historical situation that could only take place in a culture of shame. The film follows three young Irish girls who are sent to one of the Magdalene Asylums, institutions run by nuns, primarily in Ireland, to house girls who got pregnant outside of marriage, or who were considered too sexual, too flirtatious or even too attractive. They were incarcerated in these asylums, which doubled as laundries, where they worked, unpaid, seven days a week, 364 days a year, with only Christmas day off.[86]

How can such a practice, at once immoral, illegal, and inhuman, not only have survived through the twentieth century (until 1996), but have survived in the form of a public institution? Only, as Gordon puts it, because of the role of shame, both in the asylums and in the surrounding culture:

> Part of the explanation lies in the fact that the soil in which the Magdalene laundries flourished was the soil of shamed silence, the kind of silence that allows words to be spoken but makes full understanding of them impossible.

Some of this shame operated outside the asylum walls, among a populace itself humiliated by economic need and religious stricture. But secrecy also was generated by the girls' isolation:

> The laundries' existence was well known enough to become part of the vernacular, to have generated nicknames, proverbs, cautionary tales: the domestic architecture of demotic speech. Girls who were sent to the laundries were known as Maggies. There was a saying, "Bad girls do the best sheets." Children who misbehaved were told to mend their ways or they'd be sent "to the laundries with the sisters." . . . [A]ll the Irish people I have asked have said that they had no idea of the conditions of the laundries themselves. The girls were literally kept behind stone walls; invisible, isolate.

And the most telling piece of evidence is that the victims themselves were too shamed to tell the world what they had been through:

> But we ask ourselves: didn't any of the women who escaped or left legitimately (any adult male relative could rescue them) tell anyone—a family member, a friend, a sympathetic confessor—what they had endured? The answer seems to be no, and the explanation lies in the particular flavor of Irish shamed silence.

The Magdalene Asylums teach us something about corruption and vulgarity. Only when they are at moderate levels are these evils perceived as problems. When they reach extreme levels, they are accepted by whole communities as part of the fabric of life. Earlier in this book, I remarked that you cannot discuss a problem *with* the problem. Similarly, you cannot discuss an injustice with a community that has been morally diminished by the same injustice. Only sharp interference from outside, or gradually evolving consciousness within, can bring relief.

Something similar can be said about plastic prisons, which are cultural jails created by mass markets and their consumers. In Part 1 of this book, I have tried to detail how American awareness has been inhibited and debased by market forces. Constitutional guarantees of liberty remain in place, but people are denied the most precious of treasures: the knowledge with which to choose wisely. Can we remain free when our infrastructures from A to Z have been mass-produced and normalized? Does it make no difference that we pass days at a time without eating anything locally grown? That many of us cannot get by without thousands of dollars' worth of pills annually? That our children are now subject to electronic diversions from birth on? That a child can grow up without seeing a traditional village or seeing another person make something by hand?

With questions like this in mind, I must suggest that American culture is a good deal less free and diverse than it appears to be. It has pushed further and further back from nature and into an inner city of synthetic reality. It is forgetting the rush of enthusiasm that comes from direct and individual contact with work. It is growing fat and weary and depressed. And will it listen to someone who says exactly these things about it? At the time of writing, this remains uncertain.

Anthony Lane addresses this phenomenon when, in a retrospective on movie director Max Ophuls, he compares the great directors of the mid-twentieth century with the leading directors of today. He concludes that above all, Ophuls was "a man of the world":

> It is a breed that has all but disappeared from cinema, and the loss could hardly be more grievous; movies are a hothouse, and the temptation to stay inside and breathe the rot is forbiddingly strong. But some have preferred to function in the fresh air, and it shows in their

films; Buñuel was a man of the world, as were Howard Hawks and Billy Wilder, and, as for John Ford and John Huston, proudly sporting the bruises of experience, they would surely be contemptuous of any film-maker who knew nothing but film. The later auteurs could not be more retiring: Stanley Kubrick, Woody Allen, Martin Scorsese, Quentin Tarantino, George Lucas—a disparate group, yet all of them exiled or tucked away.[87]   .

Lane's statement cannot be fobbed off as pertinent to one genre of art alone: His general point can be redirected towards current American poetry, which is unreadably ingrown and obtuse, and towards "serious" American fiction, which focuses so obsessively on style that it is all paint and no barn. The arts seem to be retreating from contact with any reality outside themselves, and it is not impossible that this retreat is related to the social and economic factors previously enumerated.

Plastic prisons may strike us as harmless and even inviting, but they can be exposed by the evocation of a single vital detail. Remember Matthew Jalbert's assertion about urban sprawl (Chapter 5):

As long as it is affordable to commute long distances, to buy a large single-family home, and to irrigate a green grass lawn in the desert, people will do so. Developers will build it, and they will come.

For all their complexities, housing developments can be characterized simply and dramatically by their impact on the most basic life commodity of all: water. Imagine now that I have just driven into Newhall Ranch on a sunny California day. The middle-class residences are all well kept up, as is the landscaping. Many domestic irrigation systems have turned on automatically, as have the larger sprinklers at the school across the street. I pause, struck by an idea, and suddenly the scene is less pleasant. Back at my hotel, I crunch some numbers. If the average California water use per capita is 146 gallons a day (as of 1990), residential use alone in Centennial and Newhall Ranch must be over 20 million gallons a day: over 7 billion gallons a year.[88] I ask myself, how can county supervisors, regulatory agencies, and the press allow for such a gross increase in consumption in a state that is *already* sucking up its neighbors' water?[89] There is only one possible answer, an answer that speaks not only to water use but to urban sprawl, traffic jams, and the vanishing landscape. Centennial and Newhall Ranch are the products of a typically American conspiracy to ignore, at all costs, anything that might interfere with business.

What happens to social consciousness in a cultural prison? It becomes the responsibility of individuals: Historian Simon Schama, who chronicles the history of American unpopularity abroad. Law professor John Banzhaf, who has pioneered litigation against tobacco and fast food companies. Prosecutor Sharon Eubanks, who went after Big Tobacco and blew the whistle when her bosses caved in on the settlement. Chef Alice Waters, who changed an industry by reconsidering the role of food. Growth watchdog Matthew Jalbert, who monitors the paving-over of Los Angeles County. Literature professor Victor Klemperer, who captures a decade of state savagery for posterity. Filmmaker Peter Mullan, who draws our attention to institutionalized injustice. Film critic Anthony Lane, who achieves an insight that locates modern cinema in cultural history.

What have these observers in common? Conscience, to be sure. But also the gift without which conscience itself cannot develop: a sense of continuity and perspective that allows them to see their culture and economy in its surrounding context. We achieve this ability through workmanlike contact with the world itself and through the narratives and images conveyed to us by others. This gives us the tools to diagnose ills and isolate their causes. Continuity and perspective, moreover, bring courage: the modest stubbornness and calm of one acquainted with both trees and forest, detail and continuum.

Social Consciousness Incorporates Self-Awareness. Even the most passionate reformist zeal is of questionable value without self-knowledge. We cannot come to terms with social issues and their conceivable resolutions without putting ourselves in the equation.

Take the politically correct professors who have been dismantling humanities education in American colleges. Do they realize that they are trashing the curricular underpinnings of their democracy? Take the charismatic crusaders, like the clownish Michael Moore and the uncompromising Ralph Nader. Are they after a politics of justice or just a politics of self? We find real self-awareness in humbler personifications: Frederick Douglass detailing his own implication in injustice, Victor Klemperer opening his heart in both weakness and strength. Though Douglass was an active reformer and Klemperer but a helpless observer, both men's insights are valuable, precisely because the men put *themselves* into the mix. To do otherwise is to give no guarantee that one's vision is not self-serving and that one is not about to replace one form of injustice with another. Untempered by self-awareness, social consciousness is a self-contradiction: a heroic figure with a monster's head.

Social consciousness addresses issues, appreciates continuities, maintains perspective, and incorporates self-awareness. The socially conscious are both learned and up-to-date, both vigilant and judicious, both determined and patient, both discriminating and self-critical. With all these abilities in mind, you might almost think that social consciousness was some kind of performance art. Is practicing social consciousness the moral equivalent of playing the Goldberg Variations or making the round of eight at Wimbledon? In a manner of speaking, it is. Democracy demands these things of some people. They may at best be a loyal minority, but they will remind the rest of us what is to be loved and preserved in liberty.

CHAPTER ELEVEN

THE CONSCIOUS LIFE

One kind of writer sets out for a dinner party or other social event hoping against hope that someone there will have read his work or at least know his name. The other, more rare, wishes for the opposite. Henry James . . . belongs to the second category.

James famously described the ideal writer as someone "on whom nothing is lost," and he believed that the consummate observer must avoid calling attention to himself.

Laura Miller, *Salon,* July 7, 2002

Writing about consciousness is a little like painting the color of air. For consciousness, in its many applications, is the medium of all our thinking and writing and reading. How can we wrap a definition around the miracle of our own enablement? Yet try we must, even if we must work with bits and pieces. In the previous chapter, I looked at some examples of social consciousness and offered a conceptual model of how that sort of consciousness is formed. Now it is time to consider the conscious life. By this I mean a state of mind in which awareness reaches out to engage the world and can be refocused, without excessive bias, back upon the self.

Consciousness, as I see it, is the psychological equivalent of political liberty. If political liberty is the outward entitlement to personal enterprise, inquiry, and expression, then consciousness is the inner entitlement, the vigor of mind, that empowers these very activities. Moreover, liberty and consciousness propagate each other, depend on each other, feed off each other. Liberty engenders consciousness through example and education. Consciousness nourishes and preserves liberty through innovation and social criticism. By the same token, if either liberty or consciousness becomes endangered, the other shares its peril.

But what does consciousness do when it is *not* involved in social issues? Ought we to keep in practice by haranguing our friends, snapping at our pets, sending our restaurant meals back to the kitchen, and writing nasty letters to CEOs? A quite opposite course is indicated. The socially conscious are not malcontents who walk around displaying their open ulcers; they are instead lovers of peace and commonwealth. It is only from the standpoint of such a love that social ills or dangers may be evaluated squarely. The hallmark of the conscious life is not indignation so much as appreciation.

To understand exactly what sort of appreciation this is, we must consider human attention and the subjects to which it is paid. It would seem that the drama of human attention is played out on three levels and that only at the last and highest of these levels can the conscious life be achieved:

1. *Attention to survival.* This form of attention characterizes the thought of people who feel physically, socially, or psychically at risk. Their attention is fed into and often governed by anxiety, shame, anger, and other negatively charged emotions. It is complicated by the perceived necessity to conceal these emotions under a socially acceptable facade—an effort that paradoxically drives consciousness further inward and away from external stimuli.

2. *Attention to success.* This form of attention, which drives the modern Western economy and its global emulators, is the realm of people who can direct their emotional energies into the positive feedback loop of initiative, achievement, and satisfaction. So obviously goal oriented, attention to success drives people into engagement with the world at large, so that they can learn its vernacular and exploit its possibilities. The world that they apprehend, however, is primarily a world of means, rather than a world of palpable entities that can be explored and enjoyed in and of themselves.

3. *Absolute attention.* This form of attention characterizes what I call the conscious life. Absolute attention is not goal driven but rather derives its intensity from its subject, whether that subject is a material item, a living being, or an idea. Its mode is inquisitive, dialogic, and appreciative. To borrow a word from Martin Buber, absolute attention treats its subject as a "Thou," a presence to be engaged, rather than as a thing of use. And since it is disconnected from the imperative engines of survival and success, absolute attention sets the mind relatively at liberty to converse with the world at large.

Attention of this third sort is often discussed as an attribute of good writers. Henry James' artistic ideal was a person "on whom nothing is lost"; John Keats advocated a "negative capability" allowing the artist to dissolve his or her own subjectivity in order to take on the essence of a subject. Some literary artists are so profoundly attentive that every page glitters with jewels of perceived detail. Here is T. E. Lawrence ("Lawrence of Arabia") recounting his arrival in the Arabian city of Jeddah:

> It was indeed a remarkable town. The streets were alleys, wood roofed in the main bazaar, but elsewhere open to the sky in the little gap between the tops of the lofty white-walled houses. These were built four or five stories high, of coral rag tied with square beams and decorated by wide bow-windows running from ground to roof in grey wooden panels. There was no glass in Jidda, but a profusion of good lattices, and some very delicate shallow chiselling on the panels of window casings. The doors were heavy two-leaved slabs of teak-wood, deeply carved, often with wickets in them; and they had rich hinges and ring-knockers of hammered iron. There was much moulded or cut plastering, and on the older houses fine stone heads and jambs to the windows looking on the inner courts.[90]

Though Lawrence was known as a man of action, his consciousness was rooted in the Western literary tradition and notably in Homer himself (my Chapter 7, on Homer, uses Lawrence's own translation of *The Odyssey*). Homer is famed for his use of visual detail—detail that evokes with equal clarity the splendor of the godhead and the coziness of the hearth. Lawrence here brings his Homeric lens to bear on the vivid strangeness of an ancient Arabian city, and he intensifies this strangeness by deliberately referring to the same city with two distinct spellings: Jidda and Jeddah.

In other writings, we are treated to the very awakening of absolute attention: the birth of the conscious life. Such a birth is portrayed subtly but dramatically by William Least Heat-Moon at the outset of his travel narrative, *Blue Highways*. To Heat-Moon as narrator, the origins of consciousness are two personal disasters: his loss of a job and news of his estranged wife's new boyfriend. He is spurred to take action by the wild image of nighttime migrating geese, whose image he takes as a symbolic call to travel. He has barely set forth when he becomes alert to other images:

> Item: a green and rainy and corrupted ice over the ponds.
>
> Item: blackbirds, passing like storm-borne leaves, sweeping just above the treetops, moving as if invisibly tethered to one will.
>
> Item: barn roofs painted VISIT ROCK CITY — SEE SEVEN STATES. Seven at one fell swoop. People loved it.
>
> Item: uprooted fencerows of Osage orange (so called hedge apples although they are in the mulberry family). The Osage made bows and war clubs from the limbs; the trunks, with a natural fungicide, carried the first telegraph lines; and roots furnished dye to make doughboy uniforms olive drab. Now the Osage oranges were going so that bigger tractors could work longer rows.[91]

Torn from his customary security, inspired to strike out on his own, Heat-Moon is suddenly alert to a world of miscellaneously vivid phenomena, each as self-contained as a haiku poem yet each ramifying into a network of natural and human connections. The Osage oranges, for example, speak to him of Native American technology, of the history of communications, of soldiers in World War I, and of the changing face of American agriculture. It is his appreciative attention to such phenomena that will renew his world and give his journey its redemptive character.

Finally, there are rare instances in which, by directing our attention to detail, a writer offers *us* the surprise gift of consciousness. Here is the graceful yet aggressive opening to Eric Sloane's *Museum of Early American Tools*:

> Finding an ancient tool in a stone fence or in a dark corner of some decaying barn is receiving a symbol from another world, for it gives you a particular and interesting contact with the past. Men used to build and create as much for future generations as for their own needs, so their tools have a special message for us and for our time. When you hold an early implement, when you close your hand over the worn wooden handle, you know exactly how it felt to the craftsman whose hand had smoothed it to its rich patina. In that instant you are as close to that craftsman as you can be—even closer than if you live in the house that he built or sit in the chair that he made. In that moment you are near to another being in another life, and you are that much richer.[92]

Sloane exaggerates a bit here: You won't know how the craftsman felt unless you know *how* to hold the tool. But genius is to be forgiven such excesses. In focusing our attention on a single, simple experience—the feel of an old implement—Sloane creates a psychological revelation that is both palpable and symbolic, a direct, sudden, and surprising connection between our own humanity and the humanity of the past. Magic of this sort was Sloane's forte, as his many books and paintings testify.

The Wages of Consciousness. Conscious living returns two distinct benefits: It is exciting in and of itself, and it achieves learning. The excitement is the thrill of exploration and engagement: a thrill that is often almost childlike in its purity. This thrill and our subsequent satisfaction create a positive feedback loop, making us want to extend our attention out into the world again. The learning gained is multifarious, but often includes the strange and secret reality that broods beyond the limits of our customary cognition. When we lower our defenses, suspend judgment, and give our complete attention to something, we extend our spiritual territory, sometimes into byways new and unimagined, sometimes into areas familiar but long ignored. Either way, we learn humanity.

What kind of humanity? Precisely what people who are otherwise occupied typically ignore or forget. The details of a room, the origin of reflected light, the design of objects, our sense of belonging or not belonging where we happen to be, the habits of people who are familiar to us, what makes them nervous, what makes them laugh, the mystery of how they feel about us, the workings of nature, the things that we secretly fear or desire, the meaning of great writing and art, the creative principle, the suggestive debris of the past, the sense of a living moment. Some of these skill sets are taught in schools; some we must wring from our very hearts. Heaped together, they may resemble a shaggy miscellany, but they are the capital of wisdom, and to address them is to come about as close to the truth as we are likely to get.

This self-aware humanity can, moreover, support more active political skills: the ability to look beyond the polite exterior of human dealings, to note by a man's word or gesture that his honesty is suspect, to find within a smiling public presentation the footprints of self-interest and exploitation, to see this injustice not as an inevitable harm but as an opportunity for social action, to master the vocabulary necessary for making other citizens aware of their common peril, and to endure and counter the defensive strategies of power in all their evasiveness, dishonesty, self-righteousness, and anger. Like the abilities just mentioned, these skills are miscellaneous and complex. Consciousness is not a unified moral position so much as an array of minor arts that can, under the right circumstances, perceive and convey moral meaning. This array of arts is not bestowed or inherited; it must be learned.

The idea of learning here is critical. Again and again in Part 2 of this book, we have examined forms of learning or learnedness.

Homer's Odysseus moves through a world in which the hero's cultural literacy is set against vulgar self-indulgence. American higher education fails conspicuously to provide the sort of learning that enables students to face real-world issues. Charles Dickens' Pip (*Great Expectations*) and Joseph Conrad's Marlow (*Heart of Darkness*) go through learning curves that teach them how to engage society's moral contradictions. And, perhaps most dramatically, Frederick Douglass proclaims learning to be the only key that will unlock his slavery:

> I now understood what had been to me a most perplexing difficulty— to wit, the white man's power to enslave the black man. . . . Though conscious of the difficulty of learning without a teacher, I set out with high hope, and a fixed purpose, at whatever cost of trouble, to learn how to read.

Douglass' predicament, and his resultant resolve, should not be unfamiliar to any of us today. In the dangerous world of American Vulgar, learning is not just a good career move. It is the last best hope for a decent life.

Of course, the kind of attention and consciousness that I describe cannot be maintained throughout life or even through a single day. It is too draining, too exhausting, like a form of psychic performance art. Even to artists, consciousness is not an exclusive calling, but rather a point of departure facilitating other activities like revision, presentation, and the nuts and bolts of professional life. As active human beings, moreover, all of us must pay our dues to the two more mundane forms of attention: attention to survival and attention to success. They make consciousness possible, though we should beware lest they distract us from it.

Sharing Consciousness. Absolute attention is most highly charged when it is directed towards another person. Here the dialogic quality of the experience is multiplied exponentially by the second party's participation. The observer may suddenly become the observed: an interaction at once promising and unsettling. Can one simultaneously study another human being and reveal oneself as an object of study? The liberal rules of dialogue, with its openings for confession, laughter, refreshment, and other ways of easing tension, would seem to make this rare combination possible. Indeed, dialogue is one of the most effective venues for *generating* consciousness, because, honestly conducted, dialogue equips each participant with the other's set of analytic tools and, often enough, allows one person to share another's zest for discovery. For these reasons, dialogue can create an avenue towards self-discovery and self-knowledge.

Consciousness and Vulgarity. At the start of this book, I lionized consciousness as the only social force that could deal squarely with the various forms of physical and cultural debasement afflicting American society. It should be clear by now that by *consciousness,* I did not mean simply a whistle-blower's alertness to wrongs. Great teachers, from Homer down the line, suggest to us that the consciousness of moral wrongs is necessarily rounded out by other forms of attention: attention to justice, decency, beauty, intelligence, art, fitness, moderation, and, last but not least, humor. How this rounded consciousness confronts vulgarity will be apparent in the fable that follows.

CHAPTER TWELVE

CONCLUSION: THE HEART OF THE LABYRINTH

In André Gide's moral fable *Thésée*, the ancient hero Theseus sails to Crete to rid his native Greece of an "abominable tax": The Cretan king, Minos, has every year taken seven Greek youths and seven Greek maidens and fed them to the Minotaur, a half-human creature penned up in an extensive labyrinth. Arrived in Crete, Theseus meets with the three figures most closely connected with his mission: King Minos, Daedalus (who created the labyrinth), and Princess Ariadne. Daedalus explains to Theseus that the only means he had to keep the powerful monster imprisoned in the labyrinth was to make its interior very pleasant. Ariadne offers to pay out a long thread so that the hero can find his way back through the pitch-black chambers of the labyrinth.

Eager to destroy a ravening monster and purge his land of a national curse, Theseus makes his way deeper and deeper into the darkened prison. Nearing its center, he sees light and soon finds himself in a garden. There the Minotaur lies sleeping. Theseus is surprised to discover that the reputed Terror of Crete is in fact quite good-looking. When the creature wakes up, Theseus is surprised again: "I saw that he had no intelligence at all and realized that I was free to go."[93]

Theseus, telling the tale years later, somehow cannot remember what happened next. Did he slay the Minotaur or simply leave? Gide implies that this is just a minor detail compared with Theseus' conquest of the labyrinth and his recognition of the Minotaur's imbecility. In so doing, the author elevates the concept of heroism from violence to intellection.

Gide's message would seem to have an impact on the Judeo-Christian idea that evil is a complex or even diabolical force. Gide demystifies evil, portraying it as simple ignorance—not even ugly (the Minotaur's good looks) in itself but profoundly harmful when protected and empowered by institutional authority (Minos' decree and the labyrinth). Evil lies less in the message of a cult leader than in the cynical and self-serving machinery of the cult. Evil lies less in the tyrant than in the institutionalized abominations of tyranny. We must understand these institutions as social phenomena of monstrous strength before it is possible to weed them out.

Something similar can be said about the vulgarization of American culture. Our culture may be plagued, but it is not doomed. Our escape and survival depend mainly on our ability to perceive the cause and extent of our degradation. Our weapons lie where we have abandoned them: education, vigilant discourse and the other forms of vital communication that make democracy work. Retrieving these weapons and making them work again will make short work of the monster, for the monster is little more than our own institutionalized indolence.

POSTSCRIPT

First, a word about the important topics that I have *not* treated in this study.

I have given relatively little attention to superstition and idolatry in religion, because debating issues of the spirit is seldom a wise idea. I have spent equally brief time on sexuality, a topic that makes fools of the best of us. For fictional treatments of these two topics, see my novel about American vulgarity, *The Most Amazing Thing*.

I have omitted a number of issues that would have required lengthy and controversial expositions. These include the collusion of doctors and industry to produce a culture of prescription drugs, drug companies' suppression of negative test data, the needless and brutal act of circumcision, the congressionally condoned misuse of illegal aliens by big business, and the sanctioning of gambling monopolies for Native Americans. All these demonstrably vulgarizing practices fatten vested interests and stink of money. All, fortunately, have been topics of recent debate.[94]

When I began writing this book in 2003, the Laci Peterson murder case was in an early phase of investigation. As the Peterson case slowly lost its shock appeal, the press turned for moral nourishment to the helpless female body of Terri Schiavo, then to a charge of rape against athletic star Kobe Bryant. When those sources of public interest dried up, the journalistic guardians of our liberty regaled us with coverage of the Michael Jackson sex abuse trial, which concluded on June 15, 2005. The Jackson case was by no means a typical American trial, but it was indeed typical of what happens when American justice is stretched on the wrack of high visibility and big bucks. Numerous elements of vulgarity were well represented: a decadent, self-indulgent, and terminally gussied-up defendant; a misconceived and embarrassed prosecution; a defense whose sole aim was to demolish the credibility of witnesses, whether their testimony was false or true; and a press force freakish enough to carry on ad nauseam about the trial's events, even on days when there were no events at all. The question is, what will the networks serve up next? Will someone in the front office suggest that, after orgies of voyeurism, the press experiment with some unexplored alternative, like news? More likely, the other usual suspects—gay marriage, abortion, and priestly pederasty—will be trotted out to fill the gap until something really juicy can be found again.

THE REAL PRICE OF GAS

"The Real Price of Gas: Executive Summary"

This report by the International Center for Technology Assessment (CTA) identifies and quantifies the many external costs of using motor vehicles and the internal combustion engine that are not reflected in the retail price Americans pay for gasoline. These are costs that consumers pay indirectly by way of increased taxes, insurance costs, and retail prices in other sectors.

The report divides the external costs of gasoline usage into five primary areas: (1) Tax Subsidization of the Oil Industry; (2) Government Program Subsidies; (3) Protection Costs Involved in Oil Shipment and Motor Vehicle Services; (4) Environmental, Health, and Social Costs of Gasoline Usage; and (5) Other Important Externalities of Motor Vehicle Use. Together, these external costs total $558.7 billion to $1.69 trillion per year, which, when added to the retail price of gasoline, result in a per gallon price of $5.60 to $15.14.

The federal government provides the oil industry with numerous tax breaks designed to ensure that domestic companies can compete with international producers and that gasoline remains cheap for American consumers. Federal tax breaks that directly benefit oil companies include: the Percentage Depletion Allowance (a subsidy of $784 million to $1 billion per year), the Nonconventional Fuel Production Credit ($769 to $900 million), immediate expensing of exploration and development costs ($200 to $255 million), the Enhanced Oil Recovery Credit ($26.3 to $100 million), foreign tax credits ($1.11 to $3.4 billion), foreign income

From International Center for Technology Assessment, "The Real Price of Gasoline," report no. 3, "An Analysis of the Hidden External Costs Consumers Pay to Fuel Their Automobiles" (Washington, D.C.: International Center for Technology Assessment, November 1998), pp. 1–2. We thank the CTA for granting us permission to reprint the executive summary of this report.

deferrals ($183 to $318 million), and accelerated depreciation allowances ($1.0 to $4.5 billion).

Tax subsidies do not end at the federal level. The fact that most state income taxes are based on oil firms' deflated federal tax bill results in undertaxation of $125 to $323 million per year. Many states also impose fuel taxes that are lower than regular sales taxes, amounting to a subsidy of $4.8 billion per year to gasoline retailers and users. New rules under the Taxpayer Relief Act of 1997 are likely to provide the petroleum industry with additional tax subsidies of $2.07 billion per year. In total, annual tax breaks that support gasoline production and use amount to $9.1 to $17.8 billion.

Program Subsidies

Government support of U.S. petroleum producers does not end with tax breaks. Program subsidies that support the extraction, production, and use of petroleum and petroleum fuel products total $38 to $114.6 billion each year. The largest portion of this total is federal, state, and local governments' $36 to $112 billion worth of spending on the transportation infrastructure, such as the construction, maintenance, and repair of roads and bridges. Other program subsidies include funding of research and development ($200 to $220 million), export financing subsidies ($308.5 to $311.9 million), support from the Army Corps of Engineers ($253.2 to $270 million), the Department of Interior's Oil Resources Management Programs ($97 to $227 million), and government expenditures on regulatory oversight, pollution cleanup, and liability costs ($1.1 to $1.6 billion).

Protection Subsidies

Beyond program subsidies, governments, and thus taxpayers, subsidize a large portion of the protection services required by petroleum producers and users. Foremost among these is the cost of military protection for oil-rich regions of the world. U.S. Defense Department spending allocated to safeguard the world's petroleum resources total some $55 to $96.3 billion per year. The Strategic Petroleum Reserve, a federal government entity designed to supplement regular oil supplies in the event of disruptions due to military conflict or natural disaster, costs taxpayers an additional $5.7 billion per year. The Coast Guard and the Department of

Transportation's Maritime Administration provide other protection services totaling $566.3 million per year. Of course, local and state governments also provide protection services for oil industry companies and gasoline users. These externalized police, fire, and emergency response expenditures add up to $27.2 to $38.2 billion annually.

Environmental, Health and Social Costs

Environmental, health, and social costs represent the largest portion of the externalized price Americans pay for their gasoline reliance. These expenses total some $231.7 to $942.9 billion every year. The internal combustion engine contributes heavily to localized air pollution. While the amount of damage that automobile fumes cause is certainly very high, the total dollar value is rather difficult to quantify. Approximately $39 billion per year is the lowest minimum estimate made by researchers in the field of transportation cost analysis, although the actual total is surely much higher and may exceed $600 billion.

Considering that researchers have conclusively linked auto pollution to increased health problems and mortality, the CTA report's estimate of $29.3 to $542.4 billion for the annual uncompensated health costs associated with auto emissions may not adequately reflect the value of lost or diminished human life. Other costs associated with localized air pollution attributable to gasoline-powered automobiles include decreased agricultural yields ($2.1 to $4.2 billion), reduced visibility ($6.1 to $44.5 billion), and damage to buildings and materials ($1.2 to $9.6 billion). Global warming ($3 to $27.5 billion), water pollution ($8.4 to $36.8 billion), noise pollution ($6 to $12 billion), and improper disposal of batteries, tires, engine fluids, and junked cars ($4.4 billion) also add to the environmental consequences wrought by automobiles.

Some of the costs associated with the real price of gasoline go beyond the effects of acquiring and burning fuel to reflect social conditions partially or wholly created by the automobile's preeminence in the culture of the United States. Chief among these conditions is the growth of urban sprawl. While monetizing the impact of sprawl may prove a challenging endeavor, several researchers have done significant work on the subject. The costs of sprawl include: additional environmental degradation (up to $58.4 billion), aesthetic degradation of cultural sites (up to $11.7 billion), social deterioration (up to $58.4 billion), additional municipal costs (up to $53.8 billion), additional transportation costs (up to $145 billion), and the barrier effect ($11.7 to $23.4 billion). Because assessment of the costs of sprawl is somewhat subjective and because study of the topic remains in a nascent stage, the CTA report follows the lead of other researchers in field of transportation cost analysis and reduces the total of the potential cost of sprawl by 25% to 50% to arrive at a total of $163.7 to $245.5 billion per year.

Other External Costs

Finally, external costs not included in the first four categories amount to $191.4 to $474.1 billion per year. These include: travel delays due to road congestion ($46.5 to $174.6 billion), uncompensated damages caused by car accidents ($18.3 to $77.2 billion), subsidized parking ($108.7 to $199.3 billion), and insurance losses due to automobile-related climate change ($12.9 billion). The additional cost of $5.0 to $10.1 billion associated with U.S. dependence on imported oil could rise substantially, totaling $7.0 to $36.8 billion, in the event of a sudden price increase for crude oil.

Recommendations

The ultimate result of the externalization of such a large portion of the real price of gasoline is that consumers have no idea how much fueling their cars actually costs them. The majority of people paying just over $1 for a gallon of gasoline at the pump have no idea that through increased taxes, excessive insurance premiums, and inflated prices in other retail sectors that that same gallon of fuel is actually costing them between $5.60 and $15.14. When the price of gasoline is so drastically underestimated in the minds of drivers, it becomes difficult if not impossible to convince them to change their driving habits, accept alternative fuel vehicles, support mass transit, or consider progressive residential and urban development strategies.

The first step toward getting the public to recognize the damage caused by the United States' gasoline dependence is getting the public to recognize how much they are paying for this damage. The best way, in turn, to accomplish this goal is to eliminate government tax subsidies, program subsidies, and protection subsidies for petroleum companies and users, and to internalize the external environmental, health, and social costs associated with gasoline use. This would mean that consumers would see the entire cost of burning gasoline reflected in the price they pay at the pump. Drivers faced with the cost of their gasoline usage up front may have a more difficult time ignoring the harmful effects that their addiction to automobiles and the internal combustion engine [has] on national security, the environment, their health, and their quality of life.

PART ONE: VULGARITY AND AMERICAN CULTURE

Chapter One: The Domains of Vulgarity

1 Etymological note: My use of the word *vulgar* observes Webster's primary definition: "characterized by ignorance or lack of good breeding or taste," with the additional coloring of the Latin root *vulgus* ("crowd"), signifying "popular, in accord with mass culture." I stipulate, moreover, that vulgarity is harmful, because harm of some sort is the natural consequence of ignorant action by masses of people. The word *vulgar* is complicated, if not compromised, when it is used (Webster 3) as a synonym for *crude* and *coarse*, for crudeness and coarseness are not necessarily characterized by ignorance or in accord with mass culture. Therefore, I do not use *crude* or *coarse* as synonymous with vulgar in my text.

The distinction between coarseness and vulgarity is made brilliantly in Raymond Chandler's novel *The Long Goodbye*, where it is in fact thematic. Again and again, Chandler brings to our attention the distinction between personal integrity and vulgar self-indulgence, especially as evidenced in the major figures Roger Wade, Eileen Wade, and Terry Lennox. Philip Marlowe, the hero-narrator, is a kind of integrity tester, and he often uses coarseness as a means of testing another person's integrity or of holding on to his own. Here is Marlowe with big-time publisher Howard Spencer, speaking about the popular novelist Roger Wade:

"One of our most important authors lives around here," he [Spencer] said casually. "Maybe you've read his stuff. Roger Wade."

"Uh-huh."

"I see your point." He smiled sadly. "You don't care for historical romances. But they sell brutally."

"I don't have any point, Mr. Spencer. I looked at one of his books once. I thought it was tripe. Is that the wrong thing for me to say?"

Marlowe *does* have a point in that he is distinguishing between good writing and vulgar commercialism. Marlowe's use of coarseness ("Uh-huh," "tripe") punctuates his moral disjunction with the polite but hypocritical Spencer, and he continues in this vein until he thoroughly upsets the man. Here as elsewhere, coarseness is Marlowe's means of attacking polite vulgarity. *The Long Goodbye* (1953; reprint, New York: Vintage, 1992), pp. 91–97.

2 Hannah Arendt, *Eichmann in Jerusalem: A Report on the Banality of Evil* (New York: Viking Press, 1963).

3 Simon Schama, "The Unloved American: Two Centuries of Alienating Europe," *New Yorker*, March 10, 2003.

4 *Time* (Web exclusive), March 14, 2002.

5 *New York Times*, April 29, 2002.

6 Savage was fired by MSNBC on July 7, 2003, for telling a gay caller to catch AIDS and die. Anger, long a staple for conservatives, has recently become part of the liberal arsenal as well: "If humor doesn't bring liberals talk-show success, is the problem that they lack rage? Cal Thomas, the conservative columnist and Fox host, speaks for many when he argues that 'liberals don't have the anger' that conservatives have stored up from their years in the political and media wilderness. But this, too, is changing: Pinch most Democrats these days, and they'll vomit vituperation about President Bush as crazed as that of some Clinton haters of a decade ago." Frank Rich, "Liberals Are No Fun," *New York Times*, July 20, 2003.

7 These favors are mentioned three times in the Quran as a reward for righteousness:

And the people of the right hand oh! how happy shall be the people of the right hand! Amid thornless sidrahs And talh trees clad with fruit, And in extended shade, And by flowing waters, And with abundant fruits, Unfailing, unforbidden, And on lofty couches. Of a rare creation have we created the Houris, And we have made them ever virgins, Dear to their spouses, of equal age with them, For the people of the right hand, A crowd of the former, And a crowd of the latter generations. (Mecca, 96 Verses)

But the pious shall be in a secure place, Amid gardens and fountains, Clothed in silk and richest robes, facing one another: Thus shall it be: and we will wed them to the virgins with large dark eyes: Therein shall they call, secure, for every kind of fruit; Therein, their first death passed, shall they taste death no more; and He shall keep them from the pains of Hell: 'tis the gracious bounty of thy Lord! This is the great felicity. (Mecca, 59 Verses)

Gardens of Eden, whose portals shall stand open to them: Therein reclining, they shall there call for many a fruit and drink: And with them shall be virgins of their own age, with modest retiring glances: "This is what ye were promised at the day of reckoning." "Yes! this is our provision: it shall never fail." (Mecca, 88 Verses)

Note also the following pronouncement from the tenth-century *Arousal of the Heedless*, by Abu'l-Layth al Samarkandi: "It is related of Ibn Abbas, may God be pleased with him, that he used to say: In Paradise are dark-eyed maidens of the type called 'toys,' who have been created out of four things: from musk, ambergris, camphor and saffron, stirred into a dough with water of life. All the celestial maidens love them dearly. Would one of them spit into ocean, its waters would become sweet. On the throat of each of them is written, 'He who would desire to have the like of me, let him do the works of obedience to my Lord.'" Arthur Jeffery, *A Reader on Islam* (The Hague: Mouton, 1962), pp. 240f., quoted in F. E. Peters, *A Reader on Classical Islam* (Princeton, N.J.: Princeton University Press, 1994), p. 209.

Paradise is still presented as a literal fact in much Islamic teaching. It figured as an incentive in Atta's leadership of the 9/11 attacks: "None of the students had heard of Mohamed Atta, the man U.S. investigators suspect was the hijackers' ringleader, nor were students aware of the letter found in Atta's baggage reminding hijackers that 'You will be entering paradise. You will be entering the happiest, everlasting life.'" Tom Hundley, "Schools Indoctrinate Young Radicals," *Chicago Tribune*, October 3, 2001, www.chicagotribune.com/news/nationworld/chi-0110030384oct03.story.

8 A similar point can be made regarding commercial strategies of serving size, which, according to some experts, encourage overeating, says

Erica Goode, in "The Gorge Yourself Environment," *New York Times,*
July 22, 2003:

Rather, social scientists are finding, a host of environmental
factors—among them, portion size, price, advertising, the availability of food and the number of food choices presented—can
influence the amount the average person consumes.

"Researchers have underestimated the powerful importance
of the local environment on eating," said Dr. Paul Rozin, a professor of psychology at the University of Pennsylvania, who studies
food preferences. . . . In a culture where serving sizes are mammoth, attractive foods are ubiquitous, bargains are abundant and
variety is not just the spice but the staple of life, many researchers say, it is no surprise that waistlines are expanding. Dr. Kelly
D. Brownell, a professor of psychology at Yale and an expert on
eating disorders, has gone so far as to label American society a
"toxic environment" when it comes to food.

Health experts and consumer advocates point to the studies
of portion size and other environmental influences in arguing
that fast-food chains and food manufacturers must bear some of
the blame for the country's weight problem.

"The food industry has used portion sizes and value marketing
as very effective tools to try to increase their sales and profits,"
said Margo Wootan, the director of nutrition policy at the Center
for Science in the Public Interest, an advocacy group financed
by private foundations.

9 "Five Good-Mood Foods," *USA Today,* January 3, 1990, www.usaweekend.
com/99_issues/ 990103/990103eatsmart.html.

10 The Tuberose.com information Web page, http://tuberose.com/Fast_
Food.html, describes the physiology of sugar digestion in humans:

A 12-ounce can of soda contains about 33 grams (11 teaspoons)
of sugar. It is difficult to think that something so common, and
that tastes so good, can be so harmful to health. The ingestion of
sugar (or a high simple carbohydrate diet) actually increases uri-
nary excretion of calcium, magnesium, chromium, copper, zinc,
and sodium by impairing reabsorption in the kidneys. The loss of
calcium in the blood activates the parathyroid hormone (PTH),

which causes the release of calcium from the bones—more sugar starts the cycling that is at the root of osteoporosis, arthritis, bursitis, and gout. Sugar causes blood sugar levels to soar—insulin, secreted from the pancreas, shoots up to drive the sugar down—and rapid, unbalanced cycling ensues that eventually wears out the pancreas and makes the cells resistant to insulin—resulting in a disease called diabetes. It's no accident that it occurs in the declining years, after having inflicted so much continual damage. Sugar causes the clumping of red blood cells (as seen in live blood analyses). This impedes the flow and effectiveness of delivering oxygen to the cells and removing carbon dioxide from the cells. The result is a detrimental buildup of wastes in the body that accelerates aging. Sugar impairs immune function by competing with Vitamin C for transport into white blood cells. In turn, that reduces the ability of white blood cells to engulf and destroy invading bacteria, which leads to chronic infections. Sugar supports the growth of harmful bacteria and yeast in the GI tract which lead to not only painful and itchy infections, but, also, to infestations in the blood and body organs.

In the United States, about 50% of all carbohydrates eaten are sugar. The average adult eats 150 pounds of sugar each year. A teenager eats 300 lbs./yr.—and the trend is rising rapidly. Food manufacturers are currently deceiving the public by taking fat out of foods and adding sugar to enhance taste. It is then deceptively advertised as "fat free" to attract people who want to lose weight, but do not know that the body will convert excess sugar to fat anyway (it is estimated that 50% of Americans are overweight).

The dangers inherent in high-fructose sweetening (common across American food manufacturing) made the national headlines in early March 2004. Kim Severson, "FOODday," *San Francisco Chronicle;* reprint, (Portland) *Oregonian*, March 2, 2004, reported that the first major use of this cheap sweetener in the 1980s coincided with a sharp rise in American obesity.

A telling gauge of the relationship between overeating and mortality is the mushrooming business in oversized coffins. Warren St. John,

"On the Final Journey, One Size Doesn't Fit All," *New York Times*, September 28, 2003, says that Goliath Casket, operated by Keith and Julane Davis, has been doing a land office business:

> When Keith and Julane Davis started Goliath Casket in the late 1980s, they sold just one triple-wide each year. But times, along with waistlines, have changed; the Davises now ship four or five triple-wide models a month, and sales at the company have been increasing around 20 percent annually. The Davises say they base their design specifications not on demographic studies so much as on simple observations of the world around them.
>
> "It's just going to local restaurants or walking in a normal Wal-Mart," Mrs. Davis said. "People are getting wider and they're getting thicker."
>
> Like the airline industry, which was warned in May that passengers were heavier than they used to be, and was asked to adjust weight estimates accordingly, the funeral industry is retooling to make room for ever-larger Americans. The Centers for Disease Control and Prevention estimates that 20 percent of American adults are obese, up from 12.5 percent in 1991. Of those 70 and older—the demographic that most interests the funeral industry—17 percent are obese. Despite the numbers, nearly every aspect of the funeral industry, from the size of coffins to vaults, graves, hearses and even the standardized scoop on the front-end loaders that cemeteries use for grave-digging (it is called a "grave bucket") is based on outdated estimates about individual size.

11 Michael Pollan, "The (Agri)Cultural Contradictions of Obesity," *New York Times*, October 12, 2003, suggests that increased fast-food and junk-food marketing are directly related to agricultural overproduction: "Nowadays, for somewhat different reasons, corn (along with most other agricultural commodities) is again abundant and cheap, and once again the easiest thing to do with the surplus is to turn it into more compact and portable value-added commodities: corn sweeteners, cornfed meat and chicken and highly processed foods of every description. The Alcoholic Republic has given way to the Republic of Fat, but in both cases, before the clever marketing, before the change

in lifestyle, stands a veritable mountain of cheap grain. Until we somehow deal with this surfeit of calories coming off the farm, it is unlikely that even the most well-intentioned food companies or public-health campaigns will have much success changing the way we eat." For a more general look at the economics of obesity, see Michael S. Rosenwald, "Why America Has to Be Fat," *Washington Post*, January 22, 2006.

12 The *New Yorker* ads are from the May 26 and June 9, 2003, issues.

13 Dan Brown, *The Da Vinci Code* (New York: Doubleday, 2003); Michael Baigent, Richard Leigh, and Henry Lincoln, *Holy Blood, Holy Grail* (London: J. Cape, 1982; New York: Delacorte, Dell, 1982–1983). For the history of the Zion hoax, see Hans Speier, "The Truth in Hell: Maurice Joly and The Protocols of the Wise Men of Zion," in *The Truth in Hell*, by Hans Speier (New York and Oxford: Oxford University Press, 1989), pp. 279–293.

14 Michel Foucault's statements about Paracelsus and the Renaissance history of ideas. See Robert Grudin, *On Dialogue* (Boston and New York: Houghton Mifflin, 1996), pp. 103–108.

15 Joseph Ellis, Doris Kearns Goodwin, and the late Stephen Ambrose.

16 Laurie Goodstein, "Judge Rejects Teaching Intelligent Design," *New York Times*, December 21, 2005.

Chapter Two: Waste and Wisdom

17 Information on the number of lung cancer cases courtesy of Cancer Treatment Centers of America (www.cancercenter.com).

18 *CBS News*, quoting the *AP*, December 5, 2005:

> The lead trial lawyer in the government's landmark lawsuit against the tobacco industry, including three North Carolina-based companies, has quit the case and left the Justice Department. The move comes at a particularly sensitive time when the companies and the department could still negotiate a settlement.
>
> Sharon Eubanks, who had aggressively pursued the racketeering case against the tobacco industry, was withdrawing effective Thursday, the government said in a one-sentence filing in U. S. District Court.

Eubanks said her supervisors' failure to support her work on the tobacco case influenced her decision to retire after 22 years with the department.

Her withdrawal follows a stunning reversal in June in which the Justice Department disregarded the recommendations of its own witness, Dr. Michael Fiore, and reduced the amount it was demanding from the tobacco industry for smoking cessation programs to $10 billion. Fiore had proposed $130 billion.

After strong criticism from Democrats, the department is investigating whether political appointees inappropriately pressured the trial team to slash the proposed penalty against the companies.

"The political appointees to whom I report made this an easy decision," Eubanks told the *Washington Post.* She said her work on the tobacco case has been professionally rewarding but her politically appointed bosses "have been somewhat less than supportive of the team's efforts," the newspaper reported on Thursday.

19 National Center for Health Statistics reports that "The federal Department of Health and Human Services puts the cost of overweight and obese Americans at $117 billion in 2000, and said that being overweight results in 300,000 deaths a year." See also Kate Zernike, "Fight Against Fat Shifts to the Workplace," *New York Times,* October 12, 2003. A comparable dollar figure was provided by the U.S. surgeon general in "How We Grew So Big," *Time,* June 6, 2004.

20 See John Heilemann, "The Truth, the Whole Truth, and Nothing but the Truth: The Untold Story of the Microsoft Antitrust Case and What It Means for the Future of Bill Gates and His Company," *Wired,* November 2000.

21 The Justice Department is mentioned earlier in this chapter. For the FCC, see Chapter 4.

22 John Banzhaf, "Who Should Pay for Obesity?" *San Francisco Daily Journal,* February 4, 2002.

23 On March 3, 2004, McDonald's announced that it was phasing out a major assault on the public waistline—its Supersize program—for

health considerations. (One of the program's most noteworthy critics was film director Morgan Spurlock, whose documentary, *Supersize Me,* won the prize for best direction of a documentary at the 2004 Sundance Film Festival.) But as of early 2006, McDonald's was still engaging in an aggressive policy (TV commercials for the NFL divisional playoffs) to market outsized portions of fatty food.

24 As of fall 2003, this trend was already noticeable enough to merit national attention, as described by Kate Zernike, "Fight Against Fat Shifts to the Workplace," *New York Times,* October 12, 2003:

> Across the country, companies, states, and schools are taking more aggressive—if perhaps passive-aggressive—measures to get an increasingly overweight society to move more and eat less. The new methods go beyond putting gyms in office buildings or teaching children (or adults) the virtues of broccoli.
>
> Union Pacific Railroad has begun offering some employees the latest prescription weight-loss drugs as part of a study to determine how best to get its workers to slim down. At the new headquarters for Capital One outside Richmond, Va., the architects set the food court at the end of a string of buildings, rather than at the center.
>
> "It's a place one has to walk to," said Jim Carter, an architect with Hillier, the firm that also designed the Sprint campus. "We want people to get out of their desks and out of their offices and move around."
>
> Programs that nudge people to move more or eat better are responding to a growing public health crisis: the federal Department of Health and Human Services puts the cost of overweight and obese Americans at $117 billion in 2000, and said that being overweight results in 300,000 deaths a year.
>
> "There are times when we as a nation feel that personal responsibility is not getting the job done, and so we have to take action," said Kelly D. Brownell, director of the Yale University Center for Eating and Weight Disorders. "We could count on parents to get their children immunized, but they don't, therefore we require it. We could count on people being responsible

> and not smoking cigarettes, but we have a huge health crisis brought on by people smoking cigarettes."

25 My definition of a market as a web of information is loosely based on the work of the Viennese economist Friedrich von Hayek (1899–1992), who in two key papers ("Economics and Knowledge," *Economica* NS4 [February 1937]: 33–54; reprinted in *L.S.E. Essays on Cost,* ed. James M. Buchanan and G. F. Thirlby [1973]; and "The Use of Knowledge in Society," *American Economic Review* 35 [September 1945]: 519–530) described free-market capitalism as an interchange of knowledge.

26 Mission statement at www.chezpanisse.com.

Chapter Three:
Polite Vulgarity: American Complacency and Its Suppliers

27 Clinton and members of his administration have debated this charge, but without much conviction. In 2005 it remained a hot topic. Chuck Noe, "Aide: Clinton Unleashed bin Laden," NewsMax.com, December 6, 2001, www.newsmax.com/archives/articles/2001/12/5/153637.shtml, has this to say about the issue:

> Mansoor Ijaz, who negotiated with Sudan on behalf of Clinton from 1996 to 1998, paints a portrait of a White House plagued by incompetence, focused on appearances rather than action, and heedless of profound threats to national security.
>
> Ijaz also claims Clinton passed on an opportunity to have Osama bin Laden arrested.
>
> Sudanese President Omar Hassan Ahmed Bashir, hoping to have terrorism sanctions lifted, offered the arrest and extradition of bin Laden and "detailed intelligence data about the global networks constructed by Egypt's Islamic Jihad, Iran's Hezbollah and the Palestinian Hamas," Ijaz writes in today's edition of the liberal *Los Angeles Times.*
>
> These networks included the two hijackers who piloted jetliners into the World Trade Center.
>
> But Clinton and National Security Adviser Samuel "Sandy" Berger failed to act.
>
> "I know because I negotiated more than one of the opportunities," Ijaz writes.

"The silence of the Clinton administration in responding to these offers was deafening."

28 Maureen Dowd, "Real Hillary," review of Hillary Clinton's *Living History*, in *New York Times*, June 28, 2003, discusses the presumed promise: "Bill Clinton handed over huge chunks of responsibility to his wife on policy and appointments not only because he thought she was brilliant, but because he felt he owed her—for giving up the career she could have had to become a 'lady lawyer' in a place she didn't want to go (Arkansas), for taking a name she didn't want to take (Clinton), for assuming a title she didn't like (first lady) and for putting up with humiliation she didn't deserve (Gennifer, Paula et al.)."

29 *Publishers Weekly* review of *Mother Love, Deadly Love: The Texas Cheerleader Murder Plot* (Washington, D.C.: Carroll, 1992).

30 Quintard Taylor, *In Search of the Racial Frontier: African Americans in the American West, 1528–1990* (New York: Norton, 1998), p. 41.

31 Seymour Hersh, "Selective Intelligence," *New Yorker*, May 12, 2003, 44–51. Bracketed words mine.

32 Here the one exception was MSNBC's Keith Olbermann, who tried to keep the story alive.

33 A partial exception here is Jess Bravin, "Judge Alito's view of the Presidency: Expansive Powers," *Wall Street Journal*, January 6, 2006. But Bravin does not even mention Schmitt.

34 The standard Freudian read on depression is that it is repressed anger, that is, anger plus denial. Denial and depression figure as two of the related stages in the Kublar-Ross model of posttraumatic stress.

Chapter Four: Vulgarity, Inc.; Vulgarity.com

35 "On Leadership," in-house publication, Eli Lilly Corp.

36 Brian Morissey, "Pop-ups Work," internet.com, May 29, 2003, presents statistics about pop-ups: "While spam is the runaway favorite for top villain of Internet marketing, pop-ups consistently rank not far behind. iVillage, which banished pop-up ads from its site in August 2002, reported that 92.5 percent of its users tabbed them as their least favorite part of the site experience."

37 Rachel Konrad, "Is It Time to Stop the Pop-ups?" CNET News.com, June 26, 2002.

38 From [Frank van Wensveen], "Why I Hate Microsoft," http://www.
euronet.nl/users/frankvw/IhateMS.html. Italics added. The Web page
was unsigned but was actually written by Wensveen, a computer spe-
cialist from the Netherlands. The passage continues:

> Microsoft has always claimed that the bundling of application
> software with Windows was only intended to improve quality,
> and that consumers are better served by the fact that both oper-
> ating system and applications are produced by the same com-
> pany. Well, we've seen how that goes. Word Perfect was a better
> word processor than MS-Word ever was (read: it delivered a bet-
> ter quality of *word processing,* whereas Word only contains more
> gadgetry). But when Windows 3 was released, few application
> developers had caught up with the need to entirely rewrite their
> application code. Only the Microsoft Applications Group was
> ready. It turned out that the latest release of Word at the time
> was fully compatible with Windows as soon as it hit the market,
> while WP Corp. struggled to get their DOS-version ported to
> Windows—with an unsurprising lack of success, as they had pre-
> viously been forced to write DOS-dependency into the program
> code due to DOS's lack of decent device support. And WP Corp.
> wasn't the only one: when Windows was first released most com-
> peting software vendors soon discovered that porting their exist-
> ing DOS applications to Windows looked easier than it was, and
> that nothing less than a complete re-write was needed in order
> to produce efficient and stable code. It's also common knowledge
> that MS applications perform much better under Windows than
> competing products ever can, since MS controls the API (Appli-
> cation Program Interface) and uses undocumented features to
> enhance their own products. Compare Netscape Navigator and
> MS Internet Explorer, for example: IE hooks directly into Win-
> dows' internals while Netscape is limited to documented API
> calls. Still Microsoft denies having an unfair advantage over com-
> peting developers of application software.

Canadian International Trade Tribunal and Free/Libre and Open
Source Software, http://www.flora.ca/russell/drafts/citt.shtml, July
29, 2004, agrees: "Deliberate incompatibilities in Microsoft Office file

formats are a well known marketing tactic of Microsoft used to encourage people to abandon existing software to upgrade to the latest version of their product."

Chapter Five: Vulgarity and Nature

39 Nicholas Grudin, "Sparsely Populated Mountain Area May Be City by 2030," *Los Angeles Daily News*, June 9, 2003.

40 Nicholas Grudin, "Developer of Santa Clarita Sold to Florida Home Builder," *Los Angeles Daily News*, July 21, 2003.

41 Matthew Jalbert, *Radical Urban Theory*, http://www.rut.com/mjalbert/AntelopeValley/13.html. Here is the context of the quotation:

> Solving sprawl then becomes a regional or national policy; it must be seen in the interest of society as a whole to provide an alternative to traditional development patterns.
>
> We might frame the solution in the form a social contract, one which considers the roles and interests of capital, the government, and consumers. In order to move toward alternatives to sprawl, the consumers of housing must see it in their best interest to reject the traditional single-family home; capital must be comfortable with providing a new pattern of development; and government policies must foster investment in both the building and purchasing of these new developments. New patterns of growth are available and ready for implementation; the obstacles are, of course, numerous. As long as it is affordable.

Jalbert draws attention to "Beyond Sprawl: New Patterns of Growth to Fit the New California," prepared in 1995 by "several diverse entities led by the Bank of America."

42 I regret that the Douthwaite article quoted here has disappeared from the Internet. Douthwaite, a noted environmentalist, can be reached at richard@douthwaite.net. Ismail Serageldin is the author of *The Architecture of Empowerment* and *The Business of Sustainable Cities*.

43 Gerald O. Barney, "The Growth Model: Hard Wired and Hard to Change," Bretton Woods Project, www.brettonwoodsproject.org/article.shtml?cmd%5B126%5D=x-126-15821, June 25, 1999. Also see Arundhati Kunte et al., "Estimating National Wealth: Methodology and Results," Environment Department working paper no. 57,

Environmental Economics Series (Washington, D.C.: World Bank, January 1998); and World Bank, *Expanding the Measure of Wealth: Indicators of Environmentally Sustainable Development*, Environmentally Sustainable Development Studies and Monographs Series, no. 17 (Washington, D.C.: World Bank, 1997).

44 Kurt Eichenwald, "Operating Profits: How One Hospital Benefited on Questionable Operations," *New York Times*, August 12, 2003.

45 Ibid.

46 See note 42.

47 The intrusion of technology into nontechnical human affairs reached a milestone of sorts when, in September 2003, an NFL wide receiver was quoted on the air as admitting that he used the TV "board" (jumbo screen) to find out when a pass was coming his way. This practice, which arguably involves the unfair use of technology in athletics, is likely to be taken for granted in no time.

48 From the Crossbow and Bowflex corporate Web sites.

49 In November, 1302, Pope Boniface VIII issued the papal bull *Unam Sanctam*, in which he proclaimed Church authority over the temporal world: "However, one sword ought to be subordinated to the other and temporal authority, subjected to spiritual power. For since the Apostle said: 'there is no power except from God and the things that are, are ordained of God' [Rom 13:1-2], but they would not be ordained if one sword were not subordinated to the other and if the inferior one, as it were, were not led upwards by the other. . . .

"Furthermore, we declare, we proclaim, we define that it is absolutely necessary for salvation that every human creature be subject to the Roman Pontiff." *Medieval Source Book*, http://www.fordham.edu/halsall/source/b8-unam.html.

Chapter Six: A Footnote on Vulgarity and Crime

50 "Columbine: Were There Warning Signs?" CBS, *60 Minutes II*, April 18, 2001, www.cbsnews.com/stories/2001/04/17/60II/main286163.shtml, discusses the information that authorities had and what they did, or didn't do, with it:

A year before the attack, Joe Schallmoser and Howard Cornell were worried that Columbine was just the kind of place where a school shooting might happen. They were in charge of security for the school district that included Columbine. After the shootings in Paducah, Ky., and Jonesboro, Ark., they were afraid that one of their schools might be next.

In August of '98—a full eight months before the attack on Columbine—Cornell and Schallmoser wrote a security plan that required school officials to notify and meet with parents and law enforcement officers as soon as they learned of "a threat by any student" to "commit any act of violence." They say Columbine didn't follow the plan. . . .

After their meeting with the Browns, sheriff's deputies did warn administrators at Columbine that Eric Harris might be making pipe bombs. But according to a school district official, Sally Blanchard, the school had no reason to look into the matter further.

"The deans were told that there was an investigation under way," says Blanchard. "That they weren't to do anything. That it was informational on their part, only. So they actually took no action because certainly they wouldn't have wanted to interfere with an ongoing investigation." . . .

In February of '99, Dylan Klebold turned in a story he wrote about an assassin in a black trench coat who shoots down students and bombs the city. "The man unloaded one of the pistols across the fronts of [the] four innocents," Klebold wrote. "The . . . streetlights caused a visible reflection off of the droplets of blood. . . . I understood his actions."

Klebold's teacher later called it "the most vicious story she'd ever read," and voiced her concerns about it to Klebold's parents and his school counselor. But no school official ever looked into the matter, and it ended there. It was two months before the shootings.

According to Howard Cornell, that story gave Columbine's administrators yet another opportunity to head off Klebold and Harris—and yet again, they missed it.

In a letter, school district officials said that Cornell and Schall-moser's plan applied only "when a district employee becomes aware of a student who threatens to kill someone"—a standard they say didn't apply to Harris or Klebold.

But that's not what the plan says. The plan goes into effect when a student threatens "to kill another student or commit any act of violence." That standard did apply to Eric Harris.

PART TWO: THE CHALLENGE OF CONSCIOUSNESS
Chapter Seven: Homer and the Birth of Consciousness

51 Homer, *The Iliad*, trans. Andrew Lang, Walter Leaf, and Ernest Myers, book 2. All quotations from *The Iliad* hereafter refer to this edition.

52 Homer, *The Odyssey*, trans. T. E. Shaw [T. E. Lawrence], book 10 (New York: Oxford University Press, 1932). All quotations from *The Odyssey* hereafter refer to this edition.

53 "For other than this, that which really is I knew not; and was, as it were through sharpness of wit, persuaded to assent to foolish deceiv-ers, when they asked me, 'whence is evil?' 'is God bounded by a bodily shape, and has hairs and nails?' 'are they to be esteemed righteous who had many wives at once, and did kill men, and sacrifice living crea-tures?' At which I, in my ignorance, was much troubled, and depart-ing from the truth, seemed to myself to be making towards it; because as yet I knew not that evil was nothing but a privation of good, until at last a thing ceases altogether to be; which how should I see, the sight of whose eyes reached only to bodies, and of my mind to a phantasm?" Saint Augustine, *Confessions*, book 3.

"That evil then which I sought, whence it is, is not any substance: for were it a substance, it should be good. For either it should be an incor-ruptible substance, and so a chief good: or a corruptible substance; which unless it were good, could not be corrupted. I perceived there-fore, and it was manifested to me that Thou madest all things good, nor is there any substance at all, which Thou madest not; and for that Thou madest not all things equal, therefore are all things; because each is good, and altogether very good, because our God made all things very good." Ibid., book 7.

Chapter Eight: The Education of the Vulgar

54 Mike Carlton, *Sydney Morning Herald,* January 22, 2005.

55 "Ten Commandments Monument Will Be on Display Here Monday," Benham (Texas) *Banner-Press,* November 20, 2004.

56 On August 21, 2003, Moore's eight colleagues on the bench voted to obey a federal court order to remove the monument. The next day, Moore was suspended by Court of the Judiciary of Alabama. On November 13, a special court ordered him removed from the bench. Afterward, Moore hit the road as a public speaker and, as of late 2005, was mounting a bid for the Alabama governorship.

57 See Margaret Jacob, *Living the Enlightenment: Freemasonry and Politics in Eighteenth-Century Europe* (New York and Oxford: Oxford University Press, 1991), pp. 158, also pp. 60, 93, and 145f. European Freemasonry, whose converts included Frederick the Great, Voltaire, and Mozart, was also linked with other non-Christian movements: Hermeticism, Rosicrucianism, pantheism, and outright atheism (Jacob, pp. 36, 128, 133, 66f., 87–95). On Mozart's Freemasonry and its pantheistic implications, see Maynard Solomon, *Mozart* (New York: HarperCollins, 1995), ch. 21 and especially p. 331.

58 There are ample examples of the separation of church and state in early American history, as the following excerpts show.

Late in life, John Adams wrote, "As I understand the Christian religion, it was, and is, a revelation. But how has it happened that millions of fables, tales, legends have been blended with both Jewish and Christian revelation that have made them the most bloody religion that ever existed?" John Adams, letter to F. A. Van der Kamp, December 27, 1816.

"The government of the United States of America is not in any sense founded on the Christian Religion." Treaty of Tripoli, unanimously ratified by Congress.

Regarding religion in general, Benjamin Franklin wrote, "I have ever let others enjoy their religious sentiments, without reflecting on them for those that appeared to me unsupportable and even absurd." H. W. Brands, *The First American: The Life and Times of Benjamin Franklin.*

"As to Jesus of Nazareth, my Opinion of whom you particularly desire, I think the System of Morals and his Religion . . . has received various corrupting Changes, and I have, with most of the present dissenters in England, some doubts as to his Divinity." Benjamin Franklin, letter to Ezra Stiles March 9, 1790.

"What influence in fact have Christian ecclesiastical establishments had on civil society? In many instances they have been upholding the thrones of political tyranny. In no instance have they been seen as the guardians of the liberties of the people. Rulers who wished to subvert the public liberty have found in the clergy convenient auxiliaries. A just government, instituted to secure and perpetuate liberty, does not need the clergy." James Madison, letter to William Bradford April 1, 1774.

"My earlier views of the unsoundness of the Christian scheme of salvation and the human origin of the scriptures, have become clearer and stronger with advancing years and I see no reason for thinking I shall ever change them." Abraham Lincoln, letter to Judge J. S. Wakefield, after Willie Lincoln's death.

Ethan Allen coauthored a book called *Reason: The Only Oracle of Man* (1784). At his marriage to Fanny Buchanan, when the judge asked him if he promised "to live with Fanny Buchanan agreeable to the laws of God," Allen refused to answer until the judge agreed that the God referred to was the *God of Nature* and the laws those "written in the great book of Nature."

Thomas Paine wrote a book in a similar vein, entitled *The Age of Reason* (in two parts, published 1794 and 1796):

I do not believe in the creed professed by the Jewish church, by the Roman church, by the Greek church, by the Turkish church, by the Protestant church, nor by any church that I know of. My own mind is my own church.

All national institutions of churches, whether Jewish, Christian or Turkish, appear to me no other than human inventions, set up to terrify and enslave mankind, and monopolize power and profit.

When also I am told that a woman called the Virgin Mary, said, or gave out, that she was with child without any cohabitation with a man, and that her betrothed husband, Joseph, said that an angel told him so, I have a right to believe them or not; such a circumstance required a much stronger evidence than their bare word for it; but we have not even this—for neither Joseph nor Mary wrote any such matter themselves; it is only reported by others that they said so—it is hearsay upon hearsay, and I do not choose to rest my belief upon such evidence.

Thomas Jefferson considered himself an Epicurean (i.e., a free-thinking non-Christian). He admired Jesus as a moralist but used rough language to describe the writing of Christ's original "biographers" (Matthew, Mark, and Luke): "As you say of yourself, I too am an Epicurian. I consider the genuine (not the imputed) doctrines of Epicurus as containing everything rational in moral philosophy which Greece and Rome have left us. . . . But the greatest of all the reformers of the depraved religion of his own country, was Jesus of Nazareth. Abstracting what is really his from the rubbish in which it is buried, easily distinguished by its lustre from the dross of his biographers, and as separable from that as the diamond from the dunghill, we have the outlines of a system of the most sublime morality which has ever fallen from the lips of man; outlines which it is lamentable he did not live to fill up." Letter to William Short, October 31, 1819.

Jefferson actually edited out the religious parts out of the Bible, leaving only those passages that he deemed conformable to reason.

59 The only exception I have found is Alan Dershowitz, in an interview with Harry Smith, *The Early Show,* CBS, April 29, 2003.

Dershowitz says the document has been "hijacked. The religious right is claiming that Thomas Jefferson, of all people, the author of the Declaration, tried to build a bridge between the Bible and the Constitution." Dershowitz says Jefferson did not believe in the Bible: "He thought it was, he used a terrible word, 'dung,' to describe it. He believed that the god of the declaration was nature's god. He didn't believe in prayer."

"I want to issue a challenge to the religious right, to the Falwells of the world, to Joe Lieberman, to debate me on the true meaning of the Declaration of Independence. We should teach our children what the faith of our founding fathers really is. And the faith was in science and in reason and not in the Bible," Dershowitz says.

Yet at the same time the Declaration of Independence, in fact, invokes a creator. Dershowitz says at that time people were not atheist. People were divided into two groups.

"The big division was between people who believed that the Bible was the word of God, and that churches were the place to worship God, and people like Thomas Paine, and Washington, and Adams, who believed that God was a God of nature, that he set the world in motion, and that he didn't intervene, and that prayers aren't answered, and that was the division in those days," Dershowitz explains.

60 Gore Vidal, interview with Amy Goodman, Democracy Now! May 13, 2003. "Well isn't it pretty clear that the dictatorship is in place. We're not supposed to know certain things and we're not going to know them. They're doing everything to remove our history, to damage the Freedom of Information Act. Bush managed to have a number of Presidential papers, including those of his father, put out of the reach of historians, or anybody for a great length of time, during which they will probably be shredded, so they will never be available. And what I have always called jokingly the United States of Amnesia will be worse than an amnesiac[;] it will have suffered a lobotomy, there will be no functioning historical memory of our history."

61 Jefferson goes on: "I do not believe with the Rochefoucaults & Montaignes, that fourteen out of fifteen men are rogues: I believe a great abatement from that proportion may be made in favor of general honesty. But I have always found that rogues would be uppermost, and I do not know that the proportion is too strong for the higher orders, and for those who, rising above the swinish multitude, always contrive to nestle themselves into the places of power & profit. These rogues set out with stealing the people's good opinion, and then steal from them the right of withdrawing it, by contriving laws and associations against the power of the people themselves. Our part of the country is in considerable fermentation, on what they suspect to be a recent roguery of this kind. They say that while all hands were below deck mending sails, splicing ropes, and every one at his own business, & the captain in his cabbin attending to his log book & chart, a rogue of a pilot has run them into an enemy's port." Letter to Mann Page, August 30, 1795.

And he later returns to this topic: "I know no safe depositary of the ultimate powers of the society but the people themselves; and if we think them not enlightened enough to exercise their control with a wholesome discretion, the remedy is not to take it from them, but to inform their discretion by education. This is the true corrective of abuses of constitutional power." Letter to W. Jarvis, 1820.

"Every government degenerates when trusted to the rulers of the people alone. The people themselves, therefore, are its only safe depositories. And to render even them safe, their minds must be improved to a certain degree." Thomas Jefferson, "Notes on Virginia," 1782.

62 Sam Dillon, "Literacy Falls for Graduates from College," *New York Times,* December 16, 2005, shares his findings:

The National Assessment of Adult Literacy, given in 2003 by the Department of Education, is the nation's most important test of how well adult Americans can read.

The college graduates who in 2003 failed to demonstrate proficiency included 53 percent who scored at the intermediate level and 14 percent who scored at the basic level, meaning they could read and understand short, commonplace prose texts.

Three percent of college graduates who took the test in 2003, representing some 800,000 Americans, demonstrated "below basic" literacy, meaning that they could not perform more than the simplest skills, like locating easily identifiable information in short prose.

When the test was last administered, in 1992, 40 percent of the nation's college graduates scored at the proficient level, meaning that they were able to read lengthy, complex English texts and draw complicated inferences. But on the 2003 test, only 31 percent of the graduates demonstrated those high-level skills. There were 26. 4 million college graduates.

63 Lawrence Schwartz, "The Postmodern English Major: A Case Study," *ADE* (Association of Departments of English) *Bulletin* 133 (winter 2003), 17.

64 These are past topics of special issues of *PMLA* as listed by the parent association.

65 Jonathan Culler, "Imaging the Coherence of the English Major," *ADE Bulletin* 133 (winter 2003), 10.

66 "The humanities curriculum places primary emphasis not upon

information, important as that may be, but upon the development of disciplined thinking and writing through the interpretation of works of art, literature, or other means by which people have expressed themselves and ordered their lives, individually and socially. Courses acquaint students with poetry, drama, painting, sculpture, music, religion, philosophical systems, forms of political and social order, and historical works." Reed College Catalog, Reed College, Portland, Oregon, 2003.

67 History and Literature is the oldest Harvard concentration; for many years after the college's founding in 1906, History and Literature was the only concentration. Conceived as an antidote to President Eliot's "elective system," the concentration served as a model for the reconstruction of undergraduate education under President Lowell, who had been among the founders of History and Literature.

"The initial understanding was that History and Literature were to be studied as quite separate disciplines, but in a way that illuminated and enriched one's understanding of both. Professor Barrett Wendell, the first chair of History and Literature, insisted that writers 'could never have been what they were but for the historical forces that surged about them,' and that, conversely, it is through the literary voices of the past that the historian comes to understand 'not only bare facts but also how those facts made the living men feel who knew them in the flesh.'" *Harvard Register.*

68 The Reed College course description continues as follows:

The subject areas of art history, philosophy, political institutions, and myth are studied to understand how they and their interrelationships reveal distinctive features of Greek civilization.

Spring Semester: Rome

The second term is devoted to a consideration of imperial Rome and to the encounter between classical culture and the Judeo-Christian tradition. The course examines the background and ideology of the early Principate as developed and described by the major authors of the Augustan Age, including Livy, Virgil, and Ovid. The political, philosophical, and historical implications of this development are traced in the works of

Seneca and Tacitus. The second half of the spring semester begins with a reading of Hebrew biblical materials and then examines both non-canonical texts of the Jewish and Christian traditions as well as New Testament materials. After a detailed investigation of the confrontation between Christianity and the Roman world, the course concludes with St. Augustine's *Confessions,* in which the values and ambitions of classical antiquity are developed in the light of an emergent Christian orthodoxy.

69 Giovanni Boccaccio, *Decameron,* Day Four, trans. Mark Musa and Peter Bondanella (New York: New American Library, 1982).

70 Frederick Douglass, *Narrative of the Life of Frederick Douglass, an American Slave,* Project Gutenburg (www.gutenberg.org/files/23/23-h/23-h.htm).

Chapter Nine: Vulgarity and Consciousness in the Novel

71 Gustave Flaubert, *Madame Bovary,* trans. Eleanor Marx Aveling (New York: Harper, 1950). All quotations in this chapter are from this edition of the novel.

72 See, for example, Jane Austen, *Pride and Prejudice;* Henry David Thoreau, *Walden;* Leo Tolstoy, "The Death of Ivan Illych"; Fyodor Dostoevsky:, *Notes from Underground;* Herman Melville, "Bartleby the Scrivener"; Matthew Arnold, "Dover Beach"; James Joyce, *Portrait of the Artist As a Young Man;* Franz Kafka, *The Castle;* Thomas Mann, "Tonio Kröger"; E. M. Forster, *A Room with a View;* Hermann Hesse, *Steppenwolf;* Simone de Beauvoir, *The Second Sex;* Giuseppe di Lampedusa, *The Leopard;* and Raymond Chandler, *The Long Goodbye.* Also see David Lodge, *Consciousness and the Novel* (Cambridge, Mass.: Harvard University Press, 2002).

73 John Carey, *The Intellectuals and the Masses* (New York: St. Martin's, 1992), pp. 12-15.

74 On Hitler, see ibid., pp. 198-208.

Chapter Ten: The Nature of Social Consciousness

75 On these and related attitudes, see Taylor, *In Search of the Racial Frontier,* ch. 2, 3.

76 See David S. Peterson, "The War of the Eight Saints in Florentine Memory and Oblivion," in *Society and Individual in Renaissance Florence*, ed. William J. Connell (Berkeley: University of California Press, 2002), pp. 173-214.

77 Donald A. Norman, *The Design of Everyday Things* (1988; reprint, New York: Doubleday, 1990), p. 115.

78 Peterson, "War of the Eight Saints," p. 182.

79 Victor Klemperer, *I Will Bear Witness* (New York: Random House, 1999), vol. 2, p. 61.

80 Ibid., p. 55.

81 Ibid., p. 407.

82 Frank Rich, "The Wiretappers That Couldn't Shoot Straight," *New York Times*, January 8, 2006, explains:

> The highest priority for the Karl Rove-driven presidency is instead to preserve its own power at all costs. With this gang, political victory and the propaganda needed to secure it always trump principles, even conservative principles, let alone the truth. Whenever the White House most vociferously attacks the press, you can be sure its No. 1 motive is to deflect attention from embarrassing revelations about its incompetence and failures.
>
> That's why Paul Wolfowitz, in a 2004 remark for which he later apologized, dismissed reporting on the raging insurgency in Iraq as "rumors" he attributed to a Baghdad press corps too "afraid to travel." That's also why the White House tried in May to blame lethal anti-American riots in Afghanistan and Pakistan on a single erroneous *Newsweek* item about Koran desecration—as if 200-odd words in an American magazine could take the fall for the indelible photos from Abu Ghraib.

83 Thomas Friedman, "The Real Reasons for Going to War," *International Herald Tribune*, August 4, 2003.

84 David Remnick, "Faith-Based Intelligence," *New Yorker*, July 28, 2003. Interpolation in original article.

85 Klemperer, *I Will Bear Witness* (New York: Random House, 1999), vol. 1, pp. 394f.

86 Mary Gordon, "How Ireland Hid Its Own Dirty Laundry," *New York Times*, August 3, 2003.

87 Anthony Lane, *New Yorker,* July 8, 2002.

88 Figure for average California per-capita daily water use is from U.S. Geological Survey, http://water.usgs.gov/watuse/tables/dotab.huc. html.

89 Reuters News Service, "Calif. Moves to End Colorado River Water Wars," *New York Times,* September 29, 2003, explains the particulars of the water wars: "California took a major step on Monday toward resolving its so-called water wars and reducing the amount it draws from the giant Colorado River, largely at the expense of the state's desert farmers. Calif. Gov. Gray Davis signed legislation on Monday to implement a pact reached between four state water agencies following more than seven years of often bitter negotiations. California has been using around 5. 3 million acre-feet per year from the Colorado River but is legally only entitled to 4. 4 million acre-feet through water rights secured in some cases more than 100 years ago. Other western states which rely on the giant river, including some with rapid population growth like Arizona and Nevada, have pressured California to take less water."

Chapter Eleven: The Conscious Life

90 T. E. Lawrence, *Seven Pillars of Wisdom* (Garden City: Doubleday, Doran, 1935), ch. 9.

91 William Least Heat-Moon, *Blue Highways* (Boston: Little Brown, 1983), pp. 5ff.

92 Eric Sloane, *A Museum of Early American Tools* (New York: Funk and Wagnalls, 1964), p. 2.

Chapter Twelve: Conclusion: The Heart of the Labyrinth

93 André Gide, *Thésée* (New York: Pantheon, 1946), p. 85. Translation mine.

Postscript

94 On these issues, see Katharine Greider, *The Big Fix: How the Pharmaceutical Industry Rips Off American Consumers* (New York: Perseus, 2003); Jay S. Cohen, *Over Dose: The Case Against the Drug Companies: Prescription Drugs, Side Effects, and Your Health* (New York: Penguin, 2001);

Peter Brimelow, *Alien Nation: Common Sense About America's Immigration Disaster* (New York: Perennial, 1996); Laurence Armand French, *Addictions and Native Americans* (Westport, Conn.: Greenwood, 2000); W. Dale Mason, *Indian Gaming: Tribal Sovereignty and American Politics* (Norman: University of Oklahoma Press, 2000); Jeff Benedict, *Without Reservation* (New York: Perennial, 2002). On the suppression of test data, see Barry Meier quotation at the end of this note; and David L. Gollaher, *Circumcision: A History of the World's Most Controversial Surgery* (New York: Basic Books, 2001); Paul Fleiss and Frederick Hodges, *What Your Doctor May Not Tell You About Circumcision: Untold Facts About America's Most Widely Performed and Most Unnecessary Surgery* (New York: Warner Books, 2002). The AMA has ruled thusly on circumcision: "Existing scientific evidence demonstrates potential medical benefits of newborn male circumcision; however, these data are not sufficient to recommend routine neonatal circumcision. In circumstances in which there are potential benefits and risks, yet the procedure is not essential to the child's current well-being, parents should determine what is in the best interest of the child. To make an informed choice, parents of all male infants should be given accurate and unbiased information and be provided the opportunity to discuss this decision." American Medical Association, Report 10 of the Council on Scientific Affairs (American Medical Association, 1999). Barry Meier, "A.M.A. Adds Its Voice to Call for Disclosure on Drug Trials," *New York Times*, June 16, 2004, discusses the problem of biased clinical trials:

> The nation's largest doctors' group, the American Medical Association, adopted a resolution yesterday that urges the federal government to create a database in which all clinical drug trials performed in this country would be registered at the outset of the trials.
>
> The A.M.A. said it was taking the action because of concerns that drug industry sponsorship of such tests was affecting quality and because companies, as well as medical journals, tend to spotlight tests with positive findings, compared with those having negative or inconclusive results.
>
> "We are concerned that this pattern of publication distorts the

medical literature, affecting the validity and findings of systematic reviews, the decisions of funding agencies and, ultimately, the practice of medicine," Dr. Joseph M. Heyman, a member of the A.M.A.'s board of trustees, said in a statement.

The move by the A.M.A., which represents about a third of the country's doctors, is likely to put increasing pressure on companies to disclose more about drug trials and how they are performed. The A.M.A.'s effort comes as a group of leading medical publications is also considering a proposal to require drug companies to register drug tests when they begin as a prerequisite to having their results published. The group includes 12 major medical journals like *The Journal of the American Medical Association, The New England Journal of Medicine, The Lancet* and *The Annals of Internal Medicine.*

For over a decade, many academic researchers have called for a uniform database in which all drug trials, their objectives and their results would be registered. But only a handful of companies have voluntarily taken steps in that direction. And the Pharmaceutical Research and Manufacturers Association of America, an industry group, has not supported a registry.

A spokesman for the group did not return calls for comment late yesterday.

Under its proposal, the A.M.A. is asking the Department of Health and Human Services, the agency that oversees the Food and Drug Administration, to establish a comprehensive database available to the public.

Asked for comment, Bill Pierce, a spokesman for the department, said that while Secretary Tommy G. Thompson was interested in all initiatives that could improve health care, he and other department officials had not seen the A.M.A. proposal.

"We will have to take a look at it," he said.

The A.M.A.'s new policy, which was adopted at the group's annual meeting in Chicago, also called on review boards at hospitals, universities and medical centers that must approve research that involves human subjects to consider mandating registration as a condition of approval.

Several researchers have previously said that people who take part in clinical drug tests often do so believing that the results, positive or not, will be used to advance medical science.

The A.M.A. action follows a report by a committee for the group that surveyed the growing scientific literature that has sought to analyze the impact of drug industry financing on the quality of research in drug trials and the publication of test results.

In some instances, the report found, researchers are reluctant to submit studies unless the results are positive or significant, believing that journals will not publish them.

ACKNOWLEDGMENTS

I am grateful to Project Gutenberg of Champaign Urbana, Illinois, for making such valuable texts as *Great Expectations* and *Madame Bovary* available online, as well as to Google.com, perhaps the greatest research instrument ever created, and Yahoo.com, which backed up my files on Web pages. These services, all available worldwide and for free, made my work sustainable and affordable.

For various acts of courtesy and understanding, my thanks go to Charles Muscatine, James Mohr, Stuart Vail, John Beebe, Christopher Lee, Quintard Taylor, Ned Dana, Mark Biskeborn, Graham Hill, Gerald O. Barney of the Millennium Institute, Lili Brown of New Visions for Public Schools, and Mark Briscoe of the International Center for Technology Assessment. My agent, Robert Lescher, supported the project with grace and fortitude. I have been most fortunate to work with editors of the caliber of Jack Shoemaker and Roxy Font. Most of all, I thank my wife, Michaela Paasche Grudin, who took time from her own work in order to enrich mine, and who brought order to everything she touched.

INDEX